D1460044

LIBRARIES
WITHDRAWN FROM STOCK

Contents

Chapter 1:   *An Island Story*   5

Chapter 2:   *Pre-Christian Times*   15

Chapter 3:   *Victims of the Sea*   25

Chapter 4:   *The Kingdom of Dalriada*   29

Chapter 5:   *Vikings!*   38

Chapter 6:   *Normans*   44

Chapter 7:   *The Consolidation of the Middle Ages*   49

Chapter 8:   *The Later Middle Ages*   53

Chapter 9:   *The Sixteenth Century*   56

Chapter 10: *Troubled Times*   67

Chapter 11: *Rathlin Is Conquered*   79

Chapter 12: *Irish or Scottish?*   87

Chapter 13: *A Bloody Massacre*   92

Chapter 14: *Newcomers, and Rathlin at Peace*   96

Chapter 15: *First World War to 2013*   112

Chapter 16: *Modern Rathlin*   120

Select Bibilography   127

LIBRARIES NI
WITHDRAWN FROM STOCK

Chapter 1

An Island Story

The sea that divides Ireland and Britain is 230 miles broad. It is divided into the Irish Sea (the greater expanse) in the south and the North Channel (Sea of Moyle) in the north. Both seas can be treacherous; there are sudden changes in the weather with rough seas and strong tides. From early days man travelled these waters. Rathlin Island is in the North Channel, and Rathlin Island, like Argyllshire and County Antrim in ancient days, was part of the Kingdom of Dalriada. The Romans called the Irish Sea the Mare Hibernicum.

The Roman Empire and the Saxons did not find a foothold in Ireland, but in the eighth century the Norse sailed down the North Channel at a time when the Irish were isolated from England.

Ireland's second asset against invasion was the climate, but the Normans at length fell under the Gaelic influence, some of them becoming more Irish than the Irish themselves. Soon the North Channel was alive with ships and Irish curraghs, many sailing from Dunseverick near Benbane Head on the Antrim coast to Campbeltown in Galloway in an afternoon.

Almost exactly at one of the shortest points between Ulster and Scotland lies Rathlin Island, four miles off the coast of County Antrim and thirteen miles from Scotland; so its ownership was often in dispute. It was not only a springboard for invasions and raids, but it was an essential base for those who wanted to protect the shores of the mainland or to prey upon shipping as it passed through the straits. However, there was a lack of a good harbour.

Later, in the eighteenth century, it was molested by French

privateers, and during the Napoleonic Wars of the early nineteenth century it was used as a naval base. It was one of the essential fleet anchorages for the defence of Ireland.

Most people who live in Northern Ireland have viewed Rathlin Island many times from the north coast of Ulster. From Ballycastle its cliffs can be seen across the angry waters of Rathlin Sound. It can also be seen from Portrush. At night the red light of the lighthouse flashes across the dark seas every five seconds. The eddies meet and the tides roar. The cliffs of Rathlin are grass-topped and always beautiful.

Visitors, enchanted by the sight of an island on the horizon, will often organize a visit, but all too often because of the weather the trips have to be cancelled, and this has added to the island's aura of remoteness. Ships that sail to Scotland and along the coast of County Donegal tend to keep clear of Rathlin, for the surrounding waters are treacherous; there are sudden winds and strong tides in Rathlin Sound. However, on a calm June morning it is a delight to sail the eighteen miles to Portrush, with a good wind behind and a great green spinnaker to carry you along. If the sailor is low in the water, Rathlin appears first as two separate islands, and indeed it was divided in ancient times. The cliff to the west of the island gradually becomes clearer, and the high ground towards Rue Point rises slowly out of the sea in a separate mass to the south. Sometimes huge waves rise and then slowly subside. The crossing to Rathlin should be made with one hand on the tiller. A dangerous rock called Carrichavan lies one-third of a mile off Kinbane Head. Terrible streams pass through Rathlin Sound, and at one point strong tides can sweep the traveller directly towards the rock if there is a good wind. A reef extends from Kinbane Head one-third of the distance across the rock, but a pilot may avoid it when the flood passes along between the cliffs and the rock. On occasion a skilled captain has broken the rules and braved the 'Carrick ebb'.

Now the traveller heads north-west across Rathlin Sound. The extreme south of the island is about six miles north-west of Kinbane Head and is comprised of high tablelands about 400 feet up and surrounded by steep cliffs of limestone, analogous to the geology of the mainland. In the south there are broken cliffs, gradually declining in elevation towards Rue Point, a low rocky point roughly four miles from the mainland. In 1926 the population of Rathlin Island was 299.

A sail across Rathlin Sound is an exciting experience. Passing the reef of Clachen Bo and the white sands of Cooraghy Bay, the piebald cliff of Killeany looms. Wild flowers are everywhere, and in spring the primroses are splendid. They bloom later on Rathlin than on the County Antrim mainland.

In June, summer comes to the island. Milkweed and silverweed add their lovely shades to the brighter colours.

The semicircle of Church Bay comes into view. It nestles under high grassy banks, but in a gale the coast here is treacherous, giving rise to its reputation as a graveyard. Beyond Church Bay appears a low Georgian manor house, which had been owned by the Gage family for 200 years. The traveller can now sail in calm waters ready for the end of the voyage, but seaweed may foul the keel and there is at times a considerable smell.

An iron keel is recommended to face the waves and to avoid the rocks, but collapsible dinghies are also used.

It is wonderful to spend the night at Church Bay, and there are two piers here for anchorage in six feet of water. Nevertheless, sudden swells can come up without warning, and flood tides can break with great strength around Rathlin, especially on the western shores. Small yachts often get into difficulties in the troubled seas.

The sea air is invigorating. Seals can often be seen on their backs in the waters and oystercatchers are abundant. The smells of the seashore mingle with the smell of burning peat from nearby cottages.

I have always found the people of Rathlin friendly and straightforward, and on a visit to Rathlin I have learned startling new facts about its history. There always something new to see or do: the cliffs at Fargan Lack are alive with seabirds and their nests; events are held at a village hall; the islanders sail model yachts on the freshwater loughs (and they do this with great enthusiasm) . . . If you are lucky you will be entertained by the fireside in one of the cottages.

Rue Lighthouse is at Rue Point, the West Lighthouse is north of Bull Point and the East Lighthouse is at Altacorry Head. Many sailors have been caught in the dangerous waters around Rathlin, and not all have lived to tell the tale. Pubs provide a warm welcome and there are hilarious parties. Rathlin or Raghery men take pride in their reputation for hospitality.

Rathlin lies three miles from the town of Ballycastle, today a busy seaside resort, but the island has proved its individuality and remains isolated in spite of this proximity. The voyage across Rathlin Sound is sheltered from south-westerly winds, but the lack of good harbours on the island has deterred traffic from crossing to it in large numbers. On a sunny day the island, if viewed from Ballycastle, looks like a huge layer cake, for the white cliffs on the southern flanks are topped with an edge of black basalt. On an overcast day it looks like a pirate fortress, and in ancient times Rathlin may have been inhabited by Druids. The best place to view Rathlin is from the clear-cut cliffs of Fair Head, the nearest point on the mainland.

Rathlin is shaped like a boomerang or a great inverted letter 'L', but this is not apparent from Ballycastle. It is five miles long and has sixteen miles of coastline. The tip of the island is uneven, very like Fair Head itself. There are rocky outcrops and heathery hills with fields and cottages. Near the south end there are thirty acres of freshwater loughs. Rathlin lies in the path of all shipping sailing round the north of Ireland to or from the Clyde, Liverpool or Belfast.

Rathlin lies across the North Channel from the Mull of Kintyre in Scotland, with its steep-sided mountains. There is a lighthouse like an eagle's eyrie halfway up the slopes. To the north, twenty miles away, is the island of Islay, 'Queen of the Hebrides'. The Paps of Jura are also visible on a clear day. To the west lie the cliffs and mountains of County Donegal, and to the south in County Antrim lies the flattened hemisphere of Knocklayd, a landmark that can be seen from forty miles around.

In ancient days the sea between Ireland and Scotland was called the Sea of Moyle after the *maol* or bare hills of Kintyre.

Sailing across the Sea of Moyle on a calm day the sailor sees headlands as well as islands, and it is hard to determine where Scotland ends and Ireland begins. The sea seems more like a great lake joining the two lands rather than a sea separating them, and this is how it must have appeared to the early Irish and the Scoti who travelled freely across these waters. In summer the sea is calm more often than rough. Up until the arrival of the railway, more than 100 years ago, water united rather than separated the two peoples. Sea travel was much easier than travel by land. Rathlin was near the Scottish islands and of course stood out from the Irish mainland. It is perfectly natural that the people of Western Scotland should have wanted Rathlin to remain in Scots hands.

It was in these waters, Stuth na Maol, that according to tradition the four children of Lir were transformed into swans, following which their jealous stepmother had to spend 300 years in exile. The story is one of the great tragedies associated with Ireland. People actually believed that they could be turned into swans. According to the story, the children set out to fly from the north side of Rathlin Island to County Mayo, but they were returned to the north by St Kemoc.

Another story tells of Deirdre the Beautiful. On a rocky projection off Carrig Uisneach, just east of Ballycastle, Deirdre arrived after her return from Kintyre with her lover Naoise in the *Iubrach*, the war galley of Fergus. Deirdre was a kind girl rather than a sorrowful one. She was the daughter of Feidlimid, the bard of the Knights of the Red Branch and their king, King Conor. Cathuh, the court Druid, said that Deirdre would be a great beauty but that her children might have endless misfortunes. Perhaps she represented the growing power of the female, for whom the Celts or Gaels had a great respect.

Conor was confident of his own ability; he refused to let her be killed. He had her reared apart because he felt that she would, when grown up, be a useful member of the harem. One day she saw a calf being slaughtered in the snow. She said she could do with a calf with black hair, blood on its cheeks and a snow-white body. Leborcham was her friend, but she had many shortcomings as a chaperon. Deirdre persuaded Naoise, against his better judgement, to travel with her to the Mull of Kintyre, where they lived for some time in bliss. Naoise's brothers, Ainli and Ardan, loyally accompanied him into exile.

After a year or two Conor sent one of his supporters to Fergus to offer some kind of treaty and forgiveness. Fergus was a knight of the greatest repute and Naoise's brothers decided to dress his wound and follow him back to Ireland. A few days later Naoise, with his rare locks, high-coloured cheeks and white skin, wearing a crimson cloak trimmed with gold and carrying a sword and shield, stepped ashore with his brothers near the projecting reef of rock that today still carries the name of his father, Usnach. Behind him walked Deirdre, the fairest woman in the world, with her flashing green eyes. She was clad in saffron and was wearing a lot of jewellery. Fergus was invited to dine with a local chieftain – an invitation arranged by Conor – but Deirdre foresaw trouble. She advised the brothers to travel to Rathlin, which is described as lying between Erinn (Ireland) and Albainn (Scotland), but they boldly refused.

Upon their arrival at Conor's court at Armagh (Emain Macha) they were set upon and after a brave defence fell in battle. Fergus attacked Emain Macha, King Conor's fortress, and the fellowship of the Knights of the Red Branch was destroyed for ever.

Fergus decided to march alone on Connaught, and Deirdre accompanied him. After only having spent a year as his wife, she leaned out of a chariot while it was moving and she was killed when her head struck a stone.

Kinbane Head (White Head) lies five miles to the west of Fair Head. Carrick-a-vaan, situated nearby, is a well-known spot; the name comes from Carrick Manannan, after Manannan MacLir, King of the Sea, who was a mighty warrior ruling his house. He was as swift as a clear, cold wind in the spring. No one ever recovered after being pursued by his sword. At length he was buried in the sands off the mouth of the Foyle, twenty-five miles from Rathlin Island.

To the north of Fair Head there is a great expanse of broken water that extends east of Altacorry Head, the north-east point of the island. This stretch of dark water is called Taam MacDonnell after two of the MacDonnells, who were drowned on their way to Scotland so long ago that everyone has forgotten when it happened. A deadly tidal rip, Slough-na-more, or 'The Swallow of the Sea', erupts at the narrows between the island and Ireland. The ebb tide runs out into the Irish Sea and then west at full strength; the eddy runs back along the south side of Rathlin to Rue Point. Where the two tides meet there is a great hollow that is a danger to open boats. Slough-na-more is a beautiful sight and it may be seen from over a mile away. After four hours it subsides into a ripple, so that the sailor no longer needs to fear it. Slough-na-more and other tidal movements, like the 'Bush tide' and the 'Carrick ebb', are well known to local boatmen. There are up to seven tides in Rathlin Sound and they are a great danger to sailors.

Today with modern navigational aids there are not many shipwrecks, but in earlier days the tides brought about a lot of disasters in the waters round Rathlin. Bad weather and fog have often played their part in these disasters, and Rathlin Sound is said to be the foggiest stretch of water along the whole of the North Antrim coast.

Through the narrow gap between Fair Head and Kintyre there are only eleven sea miles and a depth of about 400 feet. A billion tons of water flows through the gap four times a day. It has been reckoned that half the power contained in these tidal movements would drive all the factories in Ireland.

Today Church Bay is the main port and Rathlin is seldom cut off from the mainland. Ushet, since it has no road, has fallen out of use as a port.

A road runs through the forest plantation above Glenshesk on the slopes of Knocklayd, and from here, a little bit to the west of Fair Head, the 'arms' of the island seem to stretch out to Ireland. Scotland is seen in the distance. However, viewed from Ballycastle Rathlin seems to be a big island. It occupies nearly half the horizon, and its black southern cliffs are like an iron curtain, hiding the secrets of its interior. Charles Kingsley likened Rathlin to a half-drowned magpie, referring to the three points on the southern face where the white cliffs of chalk glare out from under the black basalt.

The north side of Rathlin Island may seem like the dark side of the moon, but fishermen visit it regularly. There are shallows and sunken rocks, creeks, caves and crannies. From the cliffs, great ships can be seen heading across the Atlantic.

Few wild flowers adorn the southern cliffs, but an occasional sprig of juniper and potatoes grow on the cliff face. Green is a common colour here, and can be observed in some of the seaweed. For those that like bold scenery, the north cliffs are worth seeing from the water at close quarters in settled weather. The circuit of Rathlin can be undertaken in a half-day. It is best undertaken by sail. The sailor should leave with the first flood from Church Bay. There is a fair tide most of the way round Rathlin.

Sailing by the dark cliffs on the side that looks towards Scotland one can hear the tide, the noise of the swell in the deep caves, the wind whispering through the grass . . .

There are many sights to be seen on the island. Streamlets fall in cascades over the terraced precipice; choughs and kittiwakes frequent the cliffs and headlands; and at the west end of the island comes the most dramatic sight of all – the castellated stacks rising 200 feet high. In June fifteen to twenty species of seabird nest here. This community of birds has been likened to a great strident city. They are busy rearing their young. Guillemots and razorbills, single or together, spread seaward to their fishing grounds; parrot-like puffins look over their particoloured bills as they sit in wait for their prey; fulmars with motionless wings soar along the cliffs or sit caressing each other on their nest ledges; cormorants also soar around the cliffs; and shearwaters, black crosses, glide low over the water with an economy of effort. In calm weather you can see these birds 'flying' thirty feet down through the clear waters.

On the seabed around Rathlin lie corroded ships and the bones of sailors.

Halfway up the cliff on the west of the island is the West Lighthouse. The light and its dome stand at the bottom instead of, in the usual fashion, at the top of the tower, and nearby a family of wild goats can be seen grazing on tiny patches of green grass.

Rathlin Island is perhaps the most outstanding of the several hundred islands round the Irish coast in terms of the amount of recorded history and the number of distinctive features. It was almost certainly one of the first Irish islands to be inhabited by man, probably before man arrived on the Antrim coast. Stone Age man at Rathlin can be traced back some 6,000 years, and it is thought that he came across the Sea of Moyle from the Scots Hebrides.

Numerous books have been written about Rathlin. It saw about a dozen massacres in the period of the English ascendancy in Ireland, and there are more wrecks here than on any other part of the Antrim coast.

There are about forty or so horses on the island.

Rathlin is the only Irish L-shaped island, and it boasts the largest concentration of seabirds around the Irish coast, particularly in June and July when they nest on the rock stacks.

It is the only one of the islands which has a 'big house', still owned by the family who owned the whole island before the Land Acts of the last 100 years.

There have been many bloody incidents on the island through the centuries as the islanders fought to repel waves of invaders. Many of these invasions succeeded, and half a dozen of them culminated in general massacres of the islanders. Once an island stronghold is breached it becomes a death trap.

Rathlin Island was fortified about 3,000 years ago, as indicated by the ruins near the north coast of the cyclopean fortress known as Dunmore. Since then Fir Bolgs, Fomorians, Tuatha Dé Danann and Gaels have in turn occupied its soil.

The Celtic or Gaelic Church is said to have been set up on the island soon after the advent of St Patrick in the fifth century. The Church was driven out of Rathlin with the coming of the Vikings in the late eighth century.

Scots, Vikings and Normans competed with one another to control the island.

In 1551 the British Government made a move, and the next thirty-five years saw many battles and the island change hands frequently. From the late sixteenth century Rathlin's allegiance was given to Ireland, but this came to an end in the reign of King James I. In 1617, during a long and complex lawsuit, evidence was produced that dated the position on Rathlin back to St Patrick, and it was successfully argued that Rathlin was part Irish territory. The dispute about the island's allegiance is one that became violent at times – but to tell the story of Rathlin we must start at the first arrival of man in Ireland.

Chapter 2

Pre-Christian Times

The story of Rathlin is perhaps more interesting than that of any other island in the British Isles except perhaps for Iona, the site of Columba's great monastery, founded in the sixth century.

There are three major phases to Rathlin's history: the first begins with the arrival of man; the second is during the golden age of the Gaelic Church in the sixth and seventh centuries; and the third is in the wars of rebellion in the sixteenth century. This chapter must be confined to the earliest period (circa 6000 BC to AD 440).

The main sources of the Irish local history are contained in such volumes as *Leabhar Gababla* (*The Book of Invasions*), *Cormac's Glossary*, *The Yellow Book of Lecan* and *The Book of Ballymote*. These works are rich sources of local history and traditions within the island of Ireland. The histories are full of mythology and are by what Russell described as important Irish storytellers. It is difficult to tell fact from fiction with any degree of certainty. Events recorded in the sixteenth century in *The Annals of the Four Masters* are not much read, but they do contain shreds of evidence by writers who were contemporary with the Irish bards.

Another source of information is Rathlin's archaeology. It has not yet revealed a clear picture of the island in pre-Christian times, but a number of preliminary digs have been carried out and there have been many interesting finds. Of Rathlin's story in pre-Christian times there is only a small amount of evidence relating to the first 3,000 or 4,000 years of turmoil in Ireland's history.

The first men to arrive in Ireland did so at about 6000–5000 BC, long after the rest of Europe was peopled by man. Families living in the Middle Stone Age, clad in skins, came across from the Baltic; others came from Spain. Traces of their occupation have been found along the Antrim coast and in the valley of the River Bann. They supposedly had travelled across the narrow sea from Scotland. Ulster was probably the first part of Ireland to be inhabited, and Rathlin was perhaps man's first port of call in Ireland.

When the northern ice cap melted, the climate of Ireland improved as the sea rose. Sea level today is some twenty feet above high tide in those far-off times. The change, however, has not greatly affected Rathlin with its steep sides.

Life must have been pleasant for the first Ulstermen, for they would have lived in a virgin Ireland. The whole population of Ireland did not exceed 3,000 people for many generations. Organized warfare may not have been unknown. The remains of beaver and elk and numerous types of fish and shellfish have been found in middens from this period, so we know that the people's diet was a varied one.

By 2500 BC the land was approximately at its present level. Society was becoming organized and Rathlin was carrying on a valuable export trade. Axes were produced and there was a brisk trade in a hard-grained bluestone known as porcellanite, found on Rathlin in the townland of Brockley at the island's east end.

There are only two axe factories in Britain that compare in size with the one on Rathlin: Tievebulliagh in County Antrim and Langdale in the Pennines. Rathlin and Tievebulliagh axes have been discovered all over Ireland, especially on Tory Island, off the coast of County Donegal, and in several parts of England. They were used for forest clearance, for Rathlin was covered with a lot of trees in Stone Age times. The climate was mild, like the Mediterranean of today.

People in those early years did not perhaps consider themselves primitive. They lived on an outlying part of the known world, but they kept up with trends like farming and manufacture instead of hunting, which had been the only means of sustenance a few generations before. There was, it is thought, some link with the great civilizations of the Eastern Mediterranean and vessels may have traded here from Tyre and Greece. Four thousand years ago ships from Tarhish anchored in Church Bay or awaited the tide at Illan Carragh on the east side of Rathlin. Sailors would travel back laden with precious items, to places that included the Egypt of the pharaohs.

Flint can be found in the limestone cliffs – another rare material, the presence of which was of enormous value to these early generations of islanders. In the soil of Rathlin Island is found a seemingly inexhaustible supply of flint arrowheads and skin scrapers, as well as axes from many places of manufacture. The majority of the artefacts were found by chance in the days of horse ploughing. The islands of Oronsay and Colonsay, fifty miles north of Rathlin, have produced many relics of the Mesolithlic period, pointing to sailors of great ability, and perhaps there was some trade between them and Rathlin.

Rathlin islanders were in a privileged position. Everyone of importance in Ireland and Scotland would have had connections with Rathlin. Ships were eager to sell their best goods to the ruling families, who were rich enough to buy what they wanted and dominated their less fortunate neighbours.

In the summer of 4,000 years ago Rathlin rang to the 'chip, chip' sound of the axe factories.

Ships from Crete may have visited Rathlin and there appears to be some archaeological evidence for this. The Gaels travelled to far-off places, mainly perhaps in trading expeditions to Western Europe and the Mediterranean. Their influence must have spread throughout Europe 200 or 300 years before 2000 BC, to the seaports of Spain, France, Ireland, the Orkneys and Scandinavia. Perhaps one morning a small party of dark sailors dressed in skins rowed across Rathlin Sound in their curraghs, landing on the island and looking very depressed. They were traders and they brought news that a new type of axe was being sold to their customers in England. These new axes could be polished to an impressive shine, and the people that made these new copper axes are called by archaeologists the Beaker folk. They came from Spain. Copper axes were sharper and more durable than the old stone axes. They led to a decline in the island's trade in stone axes, but in Rathlin the stone axes continued to be used for another 1,000 years at least.

A change of another kind can now be seen. Soon after the inhabitants of Rathlin first heard of copper axes, Ireland was cut off from the main events of the continent. The ancient Cretan Empire, which had traded with Rathlin, now declined. It was to be thirty generations before the Atlantic sea routes spread up the Irish Sea.

From then on, Rathlin, it is certain, held a key position and was never out of touch with life in England and Western Europe. Commerce increased, but a new age of fear had arrived upon the scene.

Man looked for dwelling places that were safe from attack, and the age of the crannog, or lake dwelling, began; Rathlin was used as a large form of crannog, and gave a degree of safety from attackers from the mainland. It has many natural hillocks that might have acted as early strongholds.

The Beaker coppersmiths did not travel to Ireland themselves from England, although their axes did.

A new wave of people reached Rathlin about 1500 BC. They came directly from Spain. They were small and dark. Archaeology identifies them by their weapons, the long-headed axe and the halberd. With their supreme intelligence, superior weapons and greater wealth they quickly made themselves known. They started to work copper and utilize vast deposits of gold in the gravel beds of County Wicklow, which became the main source of gold ornamental work in Europe. The Annals called these men Fir Bolgs, which we can translate as 'bogmen and weavers of trousers'.

It is not known exactly when they reached Rathlin. Findings from the period, the Bronze Age, reveal four spears, a couple of gold cloak fasteners and some silver fibulae, or pins. In addition there are many tumuli or burial mounds on Rathlin containing skeletons in stone cists. Burial in this fashion took place in the early Bronze Age, which lasted in Ireland from about 2000 BC to AD 400. The number of these tumuli can be indicated by the present name of one of the districts, just south of Church Bay: Onig ('the place of the graves').

Islands were sometimes used as burial grounds by those who did not live on them. This is the case in the Isles of Scilly, off the coast of Cornwall. It was thought that the spirits of the dead could not cross water.

The Bronze Age men in Ulster were seamen of great confidence and skill, and this is clear from their voyages to Ireland from Spain.

The rule of the Fir Bolgs on the mainland was to be short-lived, but these early people in Northern Ireland brought fresh skills to Ulster and Rathlin. Perhaps population pressures in Europe were one of the main problems. *The Book of Ballymote* records that the Fir Bolgs were driven out of Ireland by the Tuatha Dé Danann and unsettled in the Aran Islands and Islay and in Rathlin itself. They had called themselves the Fomorians. The change can be dated to about 1200 BC with the arrival in Rathlin from England of a tribe called Tuatha Dé Danann, or 'the people of the earth goddess Danu'. They were armed with swords of bronze, and their weapons were of great strength. The change was important as far as Rathlin was concerned. All around the coast of Ireland and its islands are seen the remains of fortresses built without mortar so immense that they have been described as cyclopean, and on island fortresses like Rathlin the people made a last stand against the invaders. However, the invaders were so formidable that the Rathlin islanders did not stand a chance of survival.

Where their fortresses survive, as in County Galway and the Aran Islands, they compare with the Bronze Age fortresses that survive in Europe.

Rathlin had a fortress like those to be found elsewhere in Europe, possibly two or three of them, but little remains of them. On the Aran Islands they survived because there were a lot of stones. On Rathlin the temptation was to steal from the fortress walls, or perhaps the fortresses were pulled down by a conqueror.

In 1834 it was recorded that the island had twenty quarries in use – evidence that Rathlin was a source of builders' materials.

About 1000 BC Dunmore, sometimes known to the world as Red Owen's Fort, was built, and another fortress was constructed at Doon Bay, just north of it. There is also the smaller fort of Doon Road near Ushet. The area of Dunmore is 115 feet by 160 feet – similar to the dimensions of the fortress at Dun Formna, which is well preserved in the Inish Shea. There are also the impressive remains of Aileach to the west of Londonderry. The base of the wall at Aileach is eleven feet thick, pointing to a height of fifteen to twenty feet. In the centre there are the remains of buildings with an area of thirty feet by forty feet. The entrance was at the west. It may have taken slave labour to construct Aileach over an entire generation. A great king may have organized the building of this fortress. Perhaps he was guarding his life, but archaeology indicates that the construction at Aileach was used as a trading station.

It is further asserted that the Atlantic sea route leading up the Irish Sea had become well established by this time.

Today Dunmore makes a spectacular attraction on Rathlin. Possibly much of it was made up of white stone, which may explain the reference to the gleaming white castle in the legend of King Donn. If you want to see a similar construction, though without the white stone, visit the rounded grassy hill three miles north-west of Londonderry where the Grianan of Aileach stands as a great monument to the age, preserved almost as it was in its days of glory.

The Fomorians are referred to in *The Book of Ballymote*, and they represent another wave of invaders about this time. Traces of the Fomorians can also be seen at Tory Island off the coast of County Donegal, in the Scottish islands of Colonsay and Tiree, and again at the south tip of Ireland at Mizen Head, County Cork. The Fomorians were sea pirates and their numbers were formidable. They ruled most of Ireland during this period. There was not a subject that they did not understand, according to the ancient bards. The history of the Fomorians remains obscure, but they may have had European origins and their name seems to have been derived from the European 'Pomeranian'.

One of their legendary leaders, Conaing, built a tower at Rathlin Island which can be compared with a tower on Tory Island. The name Conaing seems to have connections with the Teutonic word *Konig*, or king.

Colonsay has a number of names which commemorate legends, like Lorg an Fhomhoir, The Giant's Footprints, and Slochd Fhomhoir, The Giant's Gully. Calliagh, the mother of the Fomorians, had one eye in the middle of her forehead. It is said that she killed a maiden whom she had kept in captivity, and she then transformed herself into a grey stone that overlooked the sea. Perhaps the Fomorians of the island are remembered in names like The Grey Man's Path, leading to The Cave of the Grey Man.

On The Stack of the Grey Man, at the west of Rathlin Island, lay the bodies of eleven grey men whose origins are in ancient times. Sloak na Calliagh (The Rock Creek of the Old Woman) at the south-west corner of Rathlin is perhaps another relic of the Fomorians.

The Colonsay tradition is in contrast with Tory Island and the story of Balor, the King of the Fomorians, who owned Tory Island. He too is reported to have had a single eye and a captive daughter. The Fomorians' religion is unknown, but Balor is perhaps a personification of Baal, the pagan sun god we heard of in the Old Testament.

The Fir Bolgs and Fomorians held their island for many hundreds of years, but eventually the Tuatha Dé Danann took over Rathlin. They in turn were conquered by the Celts, who arrived upon the scene about 400 BC, boasting swords of iron. According to legend their leader was Mil, and he gave his name to the Milesians, who were masterful and warlike. They established an ascendancy in AD 800. They were a tall race with blonde hair and had considerable artistic ability. They came by sea from France, the centre of the Celtic culture that had spread out to inhabit most of Central Europe. Tradition records their conquest of Rathlin. A few Iron Age burials have been found in the central and lower parts of Rathlin, whereas those of Bronze

Age and Stone Age occupation are mainly concentrated in the upper and the western reaches.

By the fourth century AD, about 700 years after the arrival of the Celts, or Gaels, we enter a period of history rather than traditions, or prehistory. Deirdre, mentioned in Chapter 1, was among the newcomers.

About the first century BC Rathlin was ruled by King Donn, a great guardian of the Dagda, of the prime stock of the Tuatha Dé Danann. The hand of his daughter, Taise, was coveted by the King of Norway, who had just lost his first wife. She was reputed to be the most beautiful woman in the world, with blue eyes and curling tresses. Unfortunately for Nabhogdon, King of Norway, she was given in marriage to Comgall of the Long Nails, High King elect of Ireland. She turned down his proposal. Why Taise preferred her Ulsterman to the Norwegian is not recorded – perhaps it was because of his unpronounceable name. When Nabhogdon marched from his gleaming palace, his army was defeated and he was slain by Comgall in a bloody hand-to-hand battle.

The Annals record that there was a fight between the two warriors. They fought from dawn until the end of the day.

Comgall rested for six weeks at Rathlin before he was in a condition to get married and enjoy his honeymoon with Taise. Her name is immortalized in Glentaisie, one of the nine Glens of Antrim to the west of Knocklayd, at Ballycastle. The following event is almost certainly based on a folk tradition of unsuccessful attacks upon the island. The place where Taise rested was known as the Greenan, or 'swing spot', where she sat sewing. It is one of the most attractive spots on the north coast of Rathlin, just north of Dunmore. The Norwegians fled from the harbour after their unsuccessful attack. The harbour was perhaps Doonagiall, a place where boats could be landed on the coast 500 yards north of the fort. Doonagiall, or 'the harbour of the first hostages', and Greenan both appear as names on the current six-inch Ordnance Survey map.

Another Rathlin girl of great beauty of the first century AD was Devorgilla, daughter of the King of Rathlin. She travelled to

Lough Coon (Strangford Lough), hoping to meet Cuchulain, the daring hero of the Knights of the Red Branch. All that Cuchulain wanted were two large birds flapping across the water in his direction. He immediately put a stone in his sling and hit one of them. He was always ready upon the spot. He was amazed to find two women – one of them the most beautiful girl in the world, the other her serving maid. Devorgilla approached the hero and said that it was a bad thing to have done. She said she had come to find him. He took upon himself the role of matchmaker and gave Devorgilla in marriage to his companion, Lugaidh.

As one stands upon Rathlin, snow-white swans fly past in pairs. It hardly seems strange that people should believe that among such lovely birds was a princess in disguise seeking her lost lover.

There is much symbolism surrounding historical accounts, and the island Fir Bolgs explained the great success of their masters by attributing magical powers to them. They also believed in wee folk who appeared at dusk and had magical powers.

The Sword of Light, famous in Gaelic mythology, today appears on Irish stamps. It is symbolic of the swords of polished iron that so easily overcame those armed only with bronze weapons.

Rathlin was used as an important stronghold for several thousand years in an age of fear. Many different generations looked to the island for safety, and it changed hands many times and was ruled by kings of considerable power. During at least two distinct periods it was an important trading centre. The earlier one (about 2000 BC) depended on its possession of a hard stone found only in one other place in Ireland. The later one (about 1200 BC) depended on its position at the narrows between Ireland and Scotland.

In these early Christian periods one geographer writing about the Western Isles deserves attention – the Roman Solinus. In his work *Historia Britonum*, writing in the third century, he describes the 'Hebundae'. This refers to five islands that perhaps include Rathlin. According to him the islanders lived on fish and milk, using no grain. One king ruled over Rathlin. To encourage fair rule the king was not allowed to have possessions – not even a wife. He, however, carried on relations with many of the wives of his subjects. Bede also mentions this as a Pictish practice. Whatever worthy advantages it had, it did not last. The incidence of interbreeding in a small community like Rathlin would have been brought to an end within two or three generations. The position of the king is perhaps enviable, for he had no earthly goods or domestic problems. He triumphantly ruled over Rathlin and the other islands of the western seas.

By the fourth century, some 700 years after the first appearance of the Gaels, we enter the historical period.

Chapter 3

Victims of the Sea

It is written in *Cormac's Glossary* that the waters of Rathlin roar and thunder amidst the clouds. In the fifth century there was a major disaster on Rathlin that was recorded like events in a newspaper of today.

Now comes the 'Prince of the Blood', a grandson of Niall of the Nine Hostages, a famous warrior king. He had built up a considerable trade with Scotland (the ancient Irish colonists had no inhibitions about indulging in commerce).

The curragh is a boat that has survived in Ireland over a period of at least 2,000 years. In early times the curragh was built on a framework of light willow branches covered in cow hides. A stock of butter was kept on board to grease the hides and keep them supple. This type of boat also survived in Wales as a coracle – a small, round craft built to carry one person. In the west of Ireland the long, narrow curragh is still used. Until about 1800 it was the main means of transport in Rathlin. The curragh, like the coracle, could be built of local materials and sailed through surf off a beach where there is no harbour. It has a high bow, which helps it to get through Rathlin Sound, along the shore. It's lightweight, which means it can be quickly snatched to safety on a man's shoulders. People have rowed many hundreds of miles in their curraghs on the Irish and Scottish coasts. Properly handled a curragh of twenty-five feet or more in length can brave the waves and be safe at sea in almost any weather. The crew has to be strong enough to keep the boat's head to the wind. Lightly laden, the curragh is able to sail offshore out of reach of strong tides. There must be enough sea room so that the boat can slowly drift stern first before the wind.

In recent years at Inishbofin a curragh fleet was fishing offshore when forty-four men were drowned. The Inishkea disaster occurred in 1928, when ten fishermen from that island died in a storm that blew up quickly.

Brecain's fleet can be imagined, approaching Rathlin Sound from the west with small sails of brown and white. The strong wind increased as they approached the narrows, and many boats were swamped in the great storm that developed. The sailors tried to row against the current, but the wind was too strong. All the shipping was scattered and lost; then a couple of hours later the sea was quite calm again. The disaster occurred about AD 440 (about the same date as St Patrick's mission to Ulster and the rest of Ireland).

The Annals provide us with an insight into the tide rip – a great vortex between Ireland and Scotland at the conflux of different seas: the sea which encompasses Ireland in the north-west, the sea which encompasses Scotland in the north-east and the sea to the south of the North Channel. Here the tides rush at one another.

At one time there were fifty curraghs trading between Ireland and Scotland in spite of the strong seas. The account of Brecain's fate provides us with little insight into the position of the tide. Since he was trading with Scotland from Ireland his headquarters were at Rathlin Island.

St Adomnan in his biography of St Columba, written about AD 690, refers to several narrow escapes in 'Charybdis Brecani'. One incident took place at the beginning of the voyage from Ireland to Iona, and Dr Reeves identifies the tides as Slough-na-more in Rathlin Sound. There is Altacorry, or Altracireon ('the cliff of the cauldron') on the north-east coast of the island. Also there is the name Cory (Coirre), which exists as a barony of which Rathlin formed part. By the Middle Ages the name Corryvreckan had been transformed into the field rip at the north end of the island with Jura around fifty miles away across the sea. The 'Corrie Brecan' first denoted Rathlin Sound soon after AD 440. By Adomnan's time, 200 years later, it became a general term for threatening seas in the area.

There were many Irish emigrants during this period, and they used the same name to refer to the sea between Jura and Scarba. At some point in time, when Rathlin was uninhabited, the term 'Corryvreckan' came into use, but this was discontinued when the Normans and English came to Rathlin. Now 'Corryvreckan' refers only to the whirlpool north of Jura.

It is useful to know the derivations of names. There is a suggestion in *The Battle of Comgall Clarrineat*, an early Rathlin tract of the first century BC, that Rathlin was known as Inish nam Barca ('the isle of the ships'). Jura is of Norse origin and means 'Deer Island', and was in use before the eighth century. Jura can also mean 'hope' and 'compassion'. It had excellent harbours and it was known to the inhabitants of North Antrim from earliest times.

Ptolemy, the second-century Greek geographer, refers to an island at the north end of Ireland as Ricina. He did not draw a map, but gave latitude and longitude with great accuracy, so we know the island was Rathlin. This is the only island mentioned apart from Lambay Island, off Dublin.

Pliny, a Roman, mentions Rathlin (or Ricina) in his *Natural History*, written in the first century. He also refers to what we know today as Islay. Both accounts seem to have been based on the voyage of one Pytheas of Marseilles, who sailed around the British Isles in the fourth century AD.

Islands have frequently changed names, even during the last 200 years, so it is not surprising that conflict should arise over the first sighting of Rathlin. An isle called Hinda is often referred to in writings of the early Church, but it has never been identified. Some think that it was the name for Jura; others that it was Eilean Naomh. There are four other names for islands between Jura and the north-east of Ireland which remain unidentified – Elen, Oideach, Ommen and Hoije. Rathlin O'Birne, off Donegal, appears as Inish Telling on eighteenth-century charts. Larne has had four different names – Voikings, Frith, Olderfleet and its present name, Larne – during the last

1,000 years, reflecting the fact that it has had many masters.

The tide at the north end of Rathlin has been called 'Race of Skermae', and it is now called 'McDonald's Race'.

There is a story that Brecain, Prince of Norway, asked for the hand of the daughter of the King of Rathlin Island. The King said that anyone who wished to marry his daughter must prove himself a brave seaman by lying at anchor in the centre of the gulf for three days and three nights. Brecain listened to the advice of the wise men of the age and followed their instructions carefully, putting down seven anchors on ropes made of leather. During the first night, the leather ropes broke and he replaced them with ropes made of flax; on the second night the flax ropes also broke. Brecain, however, was not to be alarmed, for the wise men assured him that ropes made from virgins' hair had never been known to fail. On the third night a few strands broke, putting an increased strain on the remainder, and at the height of the gale Brecain was swept away and drowned. His faithful black dog pulled his master's body back to the shore. There is one version of this tale on Jura, and another on Rathlin. It was now established that one of the girls had not been a virgin.

Brecain's commercial enterprise and the disaster that brought it to an end happened around the beginning of the fifth century. A few of the inhabitants of north-east Ireland sailed 'across the water' and settled in Northern Caledonia, where they became known as the Picts. Trade followed the flag, as it did for Britain in the nineteenth century. Brecain supplied his kinsmen by sea. Trade continued after his death, and Rathlin entered a period when it became part of the joint kingdom of the islands and the mainland.

Chapter 4

The Kingdom of Dalriada

St Columba had sung the praises of Christianity in North Antrim in the sixth century, and Rathlin Island heard about the birth of Christ in the East. At first the inhabitants took little interest in this historical event, but at length Christianity permeated every aspect of the entire country.

The period from the fifth century to the eighth century is a time when Rathlin was part of the Kingdom of Dalriada and at this time the Celtic Church was flourishing in its golden age.

It is useful to speculate about what might have happened if the Roman Empire had landed soldiers in Ireland. There is a story that Agricola, about AD 80, looked across the North Channel from the Mull of Kintyre and gave his opinion that Ireland could be conquered by one legion and a few auxiliaries – or a single troop. If the story is true, this great warrior must have been looking at the north side of Rathlin, at this time known as Robogdivn, the Roman name for 'Fair Head'. The unified system of the Roman Empire and the spread of Latin culture might have brought together the inhabitants of England and Ireland in a very special kind of way, with great benefits for both.

Roman merchants were familiar with Irish waters, and there seems to be evidence that there were trading stations on some of the islands – for example, Lambay Island. There has been a find of Romano-British pottery in Bruce's Castle, making a trading station at Rathlin a second possibility.

The Roman legions left Britain in AD 410. The empire had been withdrawing for a few generations before this. The men that had landed in Britain about AD 350 found themselves in a land of change and decay – similar perhaps to our own age. Established ways of doing things were being challenged. Rome, which had ruled Europe since before the time of Christ, was now in decay.

The pagans invaded Europe at a time when Christianity had permeated the Roman Empire. Fourth-century Ireland was outside the mainstream of events as invaders took advantage of the declining power of Rome, but the Irish began to invade Britain freely across the Irish Sea.

Ulster was inhabited at this time by the Scoti and their land was afterwards referred to as Scotia. The Scots that ruled the area did so from 380 to 405, led by Niall of the Nine Hostages, a great Gaelic hero of true blood. Niall was tall, fair-haired and blue-eyed. He had a reputation for military expertise, and he was known as Niall of the Nine Hostages because he said no man is a king without hostages.

The British historian St Gildas, writing 150 years after the fall of Rome, described the Scoti raids in the middle of the sixth century. The raids were so frequent that the Irish Sea is described by the poet Claudian as 'foaming with their oars'. In one great invading expedition Niall's armies seem to have occupied Britain.

Among the captives that Niall of the Nine Hostages brought back to Ireland was a youth called Patrick. At the age of sixteen he became a slave under a pagan master tending sheep at Slemish Mountain, a day's ride south from Ballycastle. Six or seven years later Patrick escaped and underwent a religious education in continental Europe. In 432 he returned to establish the Church, along with small numbers of Christians who were scattered throughout Ireland.

There were five great roads to the confederate Irish capital at Tara. They had been completed by the end of the second century under King Cormac. One of them led to Dunseverick, about six miles west of Rathlin, where there was an important port to Scotland and Rathlin. It is said that St Patrick reached Dunseverick and was entertained at the fort there. Perhaps he visited Rathlin, for he was a great traveller and sailor. He may also have visited many of the Western Isles. The harbour at Portdonoughy, the port on the east side, perhaps indicates the landing of some important people connected with the early Church – perhaps Patrick himself. In the 100 years after the coming of St Patrick, Christianity spread throughout Ireland, particularly in the north. At the same time in Britain and most of Western Europe the structure of the Church was swept away as the pagans increased in power and influence.

In 470 Fergus Mac Art, Prince of Dalriada in North Antrim, and his brother crossed the narrows between Rathlin Island and the mainland and founded the Kingdom of Argyll (the Eastern Gael). They kept their Irish names, and the emerging Kingdom of Dalriada began to take shape. Rathlin remained important for the Irish and Scots for the next 300 years.

Another Gaelic prince, today known as St Columba, was born nearly ninety years after the arrival of St Patrick. He was a descendant of Niall of the Nine Hostages and a cousin of Brecain of the Whirlpool. He founded monasteries and became the guiding light of Irish monasticism, which led to Christianity being re-established after the decline of imperial Rome. By Columba's efforts and the efforts of those who followed him the Church was established in Western Scotland.

In 563 St Columba left Derry in a curragh with twelve disciples and founded the monastery of Iona, which became one of the great centres of Christianity in the world. It remained so for 200 years. Columba obtained permission to use the island for it lay on the boundary between the Scots of Dalriada and the Picts of Northern Scotland. He obtained permission to use Iona from his cousin Conall, King of Dalriada and also King of Rathlin. When Conall's son succeeded his father, it was to St Columba and to Iona that he looked for leadership. He was crowned seventeen years later.

One of the first churches established at Iona was founded by St Comgall, Abbot of Bangor. The church was known as Teampall Cooil, or 'The Church of Cooil', an abbreviation of Comgall. There was initial resistance on the part of the islanders to the work of St Comgall. A band of thirty warriors led the way for the saint. On a second visit he was successful in obtaining a grant of land and established his church – a hut of wattles. There were pagan Druids to be converted.

The Gaelic Church took a liberal attitude in comparison with other religions, and many of its annual celebrations were derived from Druid ideas. The Celtic cross is looked upon by some authorities as a compromise between the circle of the sun worshippers and the Christian cross.

St Lugsanin founded an abbey that was more like the parish church of Rathlin, but the building was not completed until about fifty years later by Segenius, who had been abbot of the isle. 'H' was a form of the early name of Iona, and Segenius is recorded as abbot there, dying in 651. *The Annals of the Four Masters* records that Segenius founded a church in Rechrainn in 650.

Rathlin did not immediately make its name as an island monastery, though other Irish monasteries of the period appeared to be well established – for example, Inishmurray, off the County Donegal coast in the west. The site of the original church on Rathlin was the same as that of the present-day church at Church Bay – something of a rarity, for there were not more than two churches in the dioceses of Down and Connor, of which Rathlin now formed part. The Saint's Seat, a niche carved out of solid rock in a sheltered cleft on the road up the hill past the church, perhaps dates from the early period. The cleft is more in view than any other part of the Manor House Gardens, which formed part of the monastery in ancient times.

There are other early religious sites on the island, including a place called Kilroruan, the Church of St Ruan, or Luan. Leading churchmen had a hand in the foundation of these establishments, which accounts for the names. Celtic crosses appear to have been numerous on Rathlin, and the sites are still venerated; however, all of the crosses have been destroyed without trace. The best preserved of the religious relics of Rathlin is in the townland of Knockabs, situated along the west side of the island, a quarter of a mile south of the main road. There, on a high hillside among the heather, are remains of a number of circular huts, varying from twelve feet to thirty-six feet in diameter – perhaps they were of the beehive type, which was roofed with layers of overlapping stones to form a dome.

There are other islands where huts have survived intact for 1,500 years. The huts may have been simple homes, all built alike. A stone wall surrounded them, and the foundations can still be traced. These walls were not necessary for protection, and marked the boundary of monastic territory.

At Craigmacagin, south-east of Church Bay, can be seen two large granite boulders, the only granite to be found on Rathlin. They are said to mark the graves of Danish princesses. They may have been built during the Ice Age. It has been conjectured that there was an entrance to a great stone circle nearby, but there is very little trace of it today. An old map records a 'Holy Cross' in this area, but all traces of anything cruciform have vanished.

'Danes' huts', likely to have been monastic, stood east of Ushet until the twentieth century. Here they were slowly dismantled by boatmen needing ballast.

According to the seventh-century biographer of St Columba, the Saint may have called in at Rathlin. Tradition has it that he landed at Port Cam, just north of Portawillan, off the east coast.

St Columba was nearly drowned in the Slough-na-more, and Adomnan describes the sea around Rathlin as the Voltaure Brecan, where dangerous storms blew up, and the Saint prayed to God that he should not be held responsible for events on the island and upon the seas. Adomnan said he had marvellous things to tell. St Cainnech was in his monastery, which was taken from 'The Field of the Cow' and in Irish 'Aghaboe' by revelation of the Holy Spirit. He broke bread upon the ninth hour in the refectory and celebrated Holy Communion on a small table which he valued greatly. He was quick of foot, and others were left behind as a result of his haste. When Columba's ship was in peril, he called upon Cainnech to pray to God for him and his friends. After all this he entered an oratory and prayed for a little while. God heard his prayers and immediately the storm abated and the sea was perfectly calm.

Columba lived in an age of uncompromising faith. He founded his monastery on Iona in 563, at the beginning of the golden age of the Celtic, or Gaelic, Church. It was an age when nearly every island had a monastery. There were monasteries on Inishtrahull, Tory Island, Islay, Cara, Gigha and the Copelands, all of which were Rathlin's neighbours. This has been called the Age of the Saints, and it lasted from the fifth century to the late seventh century. There were signs of an age of enlightenment when the monks of Iona and in Europe recognized that the mind had a physical form. A knowledge of this period is perhaps essential to the understanding of the history of the other Celtic countries, for the writing has passed the test of time. The monks were members of the educated classes. All the monks, of course, were not saints, but the monasteries were the seat of religion and philosophy. Here history, languages, geography, architecture, farming and boatbuilding were taught. There was no gap between religion and industry.

These early monasteries were poor, unlike their medieval counterparts – poverty and labour was their rule; the monks shunned property. Money donated by rich patrons was passed to the poor. When a monastery was visited by a *rí*, or king, with his large retinue, the monks would say many prayers. The monks were austere, gentle and willing, and often had complete spiritual happiness. The cold was sometimes intense and food scarce. The Church in these early years had humour as well as self-discipline. The monks lived in individual cells, not communal residences, and the abbot lived slightly apart from his monks. The cells were perhaps made out of stone.

Within the monastic enclosure there was also a church, built of oak if it could be obtained. There was perhaps a stone altar, and some vessels. There was a refectory with a long table and beside it the kitchen. There was a library and a scriptorium, where copies of the scriptures were made by hand. The manuscripts were kept in leather satchels hanging on the walls.

Around the monastery lay farming lands with a well and a mill. On Inishmurray a monastic settlement has been preserved more or less as it was 1,500 years ago. All the building was of stone and it was surrounded by a defensive wall.

There were numerous holy occasions throughout the year and

every day except Sundays the monks wore a white linen tunic, underwear and a woollen hooded cape of undyed wool. Most clothes were black, as were the sheep of that time. The monks had the traditional Irish tonsure, which meant the shaving of the head from ear to ear. The hair was grown long at the back.

Copying manuscripts was an important part of the monks' work. Columba laid the foundation of a scriptorium – one of the most important features of Irish monasticism. Here manuscripts of great calm and beauty, balance and design and genius of penmanship were produced – the equal of any other place in the world.

Monasticism on islands is almost exclusively a feature of the Gaelic Church. Perhaps St Patrick received the idea at the monastery on the Îles de Lérins on the Côte d'Azur in France. Islands (there were plenty of them in Ireland) were a way of life for the Gaelic monks for some 200 years. The monks brought peace to the islands, an influence that obtains to this day. One can experience the presence of God on Rathlin and, of course, the other Irish and Scots islands. Rathlin was an important staging post on the journey between one monastery and another, or between Scotland and Ireland, and later between Britain and America. The monks went into exile for the love of Christ – '*Oro Christo peregrinore*'.

The Annals of the Four Masters record the deaths of the four abbots – Bishop Flannius (734), Cumenin (738), Cobthacus (743) and Aidus (768) – during the Dalriada period. They braved the weather in their quest for righteousness. Now their names are hardly remembered. It was one of the peculiarities of the Gaelic Church of those years that it was usually ruled by abbots and not by bishops. The bishop was one of the officers of the abbey. Control was by individuals, and the system carried with it the seeds of its own destruction, for there was no definite central authority. The Synod of Whitby was held in 690 at the period when the Irish Church was in decline, giving way to foreign ministers like St Augustine, who were partly drawn from Europe.

Little has been written about the temporal background for those who ruled on their own islands when there was a flowering of Christianity in Ireland/Ulster and the Scots islands. There are many mentions of the Kings of Dalriada in *The Annals of Ulster*, which reveal battles and deaths, but Rathlin is not mentioned. The warriors bypassed the island on their raids, and often landed at Murlough Bay, a few miles south-east of Fair Head. Today Murlough Bay is not much used as a harbour, but it has earned the name 'Dalreti of Muirbolg', the Irish half of the Kingdom of Dalriada.

An end to pagan Ulster typifies the period. It was said that soldiers swore by their swords, especially Connaught men. Warriors would plunder every night, and they would sleep with their swords at the ready. In 621 Conaig, son of Aedhan, was drowned and the chroniclers sang his praises.

There were many sea routes to Rathlin. In 734 Flaithbertagh led his fleet to Ulster and there was great slaughter on the island of Hoine; many men were drowned in the River Bann. Hoine is usually identified as an uninhabited island, along with Moine. It is perhaps possible that Rathlin was sometimes called Moine, or 'Isle of the Monks' at this period. It is the only sizeable island near the River Bann, and a shortage of references to Rathlin suggests that the island may have had another name. The name of Iona was the result perhaps of what may be called a clerical error. Iona was originally called 'I' or 'Ai'. In Latin Rathlin is spelled and referred to as Iona. Iona is one of the most beautiful names in the English language.

Kingship was not always respected. In 736 the King of Dalriada, Oingus, seized Brude, King of the Picts. There was slaughter in County Donegal as an act of revenge. In 870 the great fortress of Dunseverick was sacked for the first time ever, but there was no move to attack Rathlin. Ireland in these years was known as Scotia or Evernia, and its people were known as the Scots. Those who left Ulster to settle in Southern Scotland were called children of Dalriada or Alba. People returning to Alba began to use the word 'Britain'. In the southern half of Scotland the title 'The Kingdom of Dalriada' was used. The activities of the Picts of Northern Alba and the people of the Kingdom of Strathclyde were still threatening from the north and the south respectively. This is an obscure period of Scots history, but it appears that, about 750, the communities of Irish and Scottish Dalriada were drifting apart.

During this lengthy period the monasteries lost some of their simplicity. As successive kings died, their gifts of gold cups, jewellery and plate passed to the Church. In the small, dark churches the altars and pictures of the saints must have gleamed with silver and gold, wrought in intricate designs. The Church was becoming rich.

Chapter 5

Vikings!

By the end of the eighth century Rathlin had already been inhabited for thousands of years, but life was still simple on the islands. On the mainland there were wars and rumours of wars – battles, burnings and murders – but the monks were sufficiently isolated from their enemies. In battles between local kings, monasteries were not generally considered to be fair game; they were said to possess magical powers.

In 793 a powerful Viking or Norse fleet appeared off the shore of Lindisfarne, in England. Many monks were killed, and the Vikings captured all the cattle. They sailed away with rich hoards of gold, jewels and other sacred objects. The heathen Vikings broke the rules of warfare, and news of their atrocities travelled abroad. Not only in England, but all over Ireland, news spread that the Vikings ruled the seas.

The monks on Rathlin were ever vigilant and hoped that their island should be spared; but one day long high-prowed ships sailed on to the beaches at Church Bay. There was little the monks could do to protect themselves, but they were not averse to taking up arms in self-defence. It was reported in Latin that Rathlin was set alight by pirates from overseas and the shrines destroyed.

Iona was raided in the next year, and three times in the following decade. The monastery was burnt down in 812, but the monks returned and rebuilt the precious shrines. They were somewhat successful in hiding their belongings from the Vikings before they arrived. By 810 it was decided to abandon Iona and shift the relics to Kells in County Meath, where the monks built themselves a headquarters. Despite their vigilance, the monastery at Kildare was sacked sixteen times during the next 100 years and those at Armagh and Clonmacnoise eleven and twelve times respectively. The death of Abbot Freadacus, the son of Sergius, is recorded.

Fifty years after their first raid the Norse were still active on Rathlin Island, but the Rathlin monks had acquired a reputation for putting up a strong resistance. Rathlin monastery survived when on other islands the monks had been slain. In 924 the Vikings sailed into Rathlin Sound to take Dunseverick (Dun Severich), but it appears that they did not sack Rathlin.

Records are perhaps incomplete, but it was not until 973, 180 years after the first raids, that *The Annals of Ulster* make reference to further slaughter upon Rathlin. In that year there were terrible deeds and many of the monks were carried off into slavery.

The chanting of monks and their preoccupation with spiritual matters can be annoying if one is not religious, so perhaps we can have some sympathy with the Vikings! The monks were resolute in their faith despite these attacks by large numbers of Vikings. In their own way the monks of Rathlin had overrun the Antichrist, the ravages of the pagans and at a later date the Normans.

From the ninth century the Scots islands were a separate political entity, known to the Irish as Inisgal (The Isles of the Foreigners). The Vikings had raided the Sudreys or South Islands, which compromised all of the Hebrides and the Isle of Man – a name that survives today in the fifth bishopric of Sodor and Man. At the same time the Orkneys and the Shetlands were known as the Nordreys.

There is very little written evidence that Rathlin was occupied by the Norse. The word 'Bo' (the Clacken Bo, the Bo Reef in Church Bay) appears to be the only 'evidence' available. No Viking burial mounds have been found to compare with those excavated on Colonsay, where a chieftain was interred with his wife and his ship. Perhaps all linguistic traces, and the blue eyes and fair hair of the people of Viking blood, were obliterated in the sixteenth-century massacres.

However, Rathlin may not have been entirely overlooked by the Norse, for it is a stronghold at the entrance to the Irish Sea. When ships were held up by the tides that prevailed between Scotland and Ireland, they would have to rest at Rathlin until they could make headway. The Norsemen did not seem to have mentioned Rathlin by name in the Nordic writings of the period.

A vivid description of Viking activity is contained in *The Saga of Burnt Njal*, as translated by Sir George Dascent. This is a family blood feud sparked by a woman's jealousy. One chapter records how Njal's sons, Grim and Helgo, sailed from Ireland in a trading vessel hoping to reach Scotland. They were driven south by a strong wind from the north; but there was a thick mist, so they could not tell whither they were driven. At last they came to where great seas were running. They thought they were near land. The pilot said that there were many tides here that sailors might struggle with. Two nights later they saw great walls of surf running up the firth. They cast anchor outside the breakers, and the wind fell until there was calm.

Thirteen ships were seen coming out to demand the surrender of their goods and of their lives, but Helgo persuaded the chapmen, or traders, to fight even against these odds. Men were killed on both sides. Then they saw ships coming from the south – not fewer than ten. They rowed hard and steered with great care. There were shields by their sides and there was a man at the mast clad in silk and wearing a golden helm. He had a spear inlaid with gold in his hand. Helgo had reached the enemy, who were Gritgard and Snowcolf. Helgo asked who the newcomers were and they said their leader's name was Kari and they came in peace. Helgo at this said they were welcome and that they could give him a little help. They said they would provide all the help that was needed. Helgo said that they must fall upon his enemies.

The battle began a second time, and when they had fought for a while Kari sprang upon Snowcolf's ship. Snowcolf turned to meet him, to smite him with his sword. Kari leaped backwards and Snowcolf cut the beam. Kari's sword now fell on Snowcolf's shoulder. The stroke was so great that it cut off half of his shoulder and arm. Snowcolf met his death there and then. Gritgard brandished a spear and sprang up, but the spear missed Kari. Just then Helgo and Grim came up. Helgo sprang on Gritgard and thrust his spear through him – a death blow. After this they went around the whole ship, and the men begged for mercy. Peace was declared.

Kari was one of the bodyguards of Earl Sigurd, ruler of all the Irish and Scottish islands, and he had been busy gathering tributes in the southern isles, including Rathlin Island, from Earl Gilla.

When they next met it was spring and Kari asked Njal's sons to engage in combat with him, but Grim said he would do so only if Kari would later sail with them out to Iceland. Kari gave his word to do that and they joined him in sea roving. They sailed south to Anglesey and all the southern isles. They headed to Kintyre. They landed their crew and obtained many goods, at length heading back to their ships. They sailed south to Wales; then they went as far as the Isle of Man, where they met Godred, and slew his friend Dungal, the Viking's son, and took great spoil. They headed on north to Kola (Colla) and found Earl Gilla there and greeted him; they stayed with him for a while. The Earl went with them to the Orkneys to meet Earl Sigurd. Next spring Sigurd gave away his sister Nereiden to Earl Gilla, and they headed back to the southern isles.

Kari's raid took place about 980 – that is, roughly the same period as the second raid on Rathlin, described in *The Annals of the Four Masters*. The men of Rathlin watched for the coming of the Danes at the high point of the road to the west, near where the Forestry Commission land is now, and when they saw them coming they would run to the west end of the island and climb to the top of Dunmore, a big rock near the Bull. They would wait there until the Danes had departed. However, on one occasion they were asleep when the Danes arrived, and they were put to death. They were buried in the heather with thorns on their heads. It was said to be unlucky to touch the thorn bushes, but a few years ago a boy pulled out a thorn for the devilment of it, and he died a few days later. He was climbing up the cliffs, looking for seabirds' eggs, when the rope broke.

The Viking incursions mellowed, and the civil war of the Gaels began. In 1018 a force of Vikings assisted King Conor at the Battle of Ulfrek's Fjord at Larne against the Earl of Orkney. In 1036 the Irish headed for Scotland to assist Earl Muddan against Thornfinn in a battle.

Sigurd the Stout, Kari's leader, lord of all the Irish and Scottish islands, was killed at the Battle of Clontarf in 1014. This was the most decisive defeat of the Vikings in Ireland. Death troubled the seas around pagan Ireland. Dublin was put back into the hands of the Irish, but a little Viking power remained in Ireland for another 200 years at least.

Sigurd, like his successor, Thornfinn, was also Lord of the Isles. He probably landed at Rathlin, but the MacQuillans, lords of North-East Ulster, seem to have had some kind of control over the island. In 1038 Rancal Eochada, their king, fought the Norse under Imar, who was the son of Harold, who had been killed at the Battle of Clontarf. The Norse flag of the raven brought victory that day, but 300 of Imar's men were slain. This is the last recorded Viking raid on Rathlin. At last there was peace for the monks. There is no record of any regular religious service on the island for 700 years.

Magnus Barefoot, King of Norway from 1093 to 1103, had a typical Viking temperament and reinforced the authority of the Norwegian Crown over the Scottish and Irish islands. He anchored his boat inside the Skerries, off Portrush, in 1103 and fought an important battle in the sandhills in a place still called The War Hollow. He died fighting in Ulster in the same year.

Many of the Scots islands paid tribute to the King of Norway in this period. In 1266, King Haakon was beaten at the Battle of Largs by Alexander, King of Scotland. There was a truce during which the Norwegians handed over to the Scots the overlordship of the Isle of Man and all the Sudreys in return for a tribute of 4,000 marks. This brought to an end the period of Viking rule of the islands.

Rathlin was excluded from this arrangement, for it was now finally Anglo-Norman. Whether it was part of the Kingdom of Ireland or part of Scotland was now disputed for many centuries. The Church grew under the diocesan system in the Ireland of the Normans. Spiritual duties were left with the Bishop of Connor, but there is little evidence that he took his duties seriously.

Chapter 6

Normans

The Manx Chronicle states that the Kingdom of the Isles was ruled for a time by the sons of Somerled, who took possession of Rathlin. Soon after, in 1100, a child was born to him in Argyll and he too was given the Norse name of Somerled. After a struggle he became a great chieftain, or thane. He was perhaps descended on his mother's side from Sigurd the Stout, the Orkney earl. Somerled raised the standard of revolt against the Normans of the Isles. In 1156 he met them in a great fight on the night of Epiphany. There were heavy losses on both sides and neither could claim victory. In the morning peace was declared and the Kingdom of the Isles was divided between Somerled's sons, Dugald and Godred, the Viking Kings of the Isle of Man. Dugald took Kintyre, Bute and the Sudreys, including Rathlin. Godred retained Man, Arran and the Nordreys. The Isle of Man sea empire was cut in two. In 1664 Somerled was assassinated, and Godred for a time came into possession of all the islands with the exception of the Isle of Skye and Bute. From Somerled's son Donald descended the MacDonnells of the Isles.

The land boundary of Ireland was always changing, in favour of either Scotland or Ulster. There was perhaps warfare between one chief and another. The strong central authority of the feudal system might have brought peace, power and authority to all. However, the Irish still robbed the country of wealth. They were unable to live in peace with one another.

The Normans had a considerable reputation as a warrior race. During the previous three generations they had subdued

England and Wales, and sooner or later they would be asked to come on to the side of the military in Ireland in this 1,000-year war. The Normans held Wexford in the south of Ireland in 1169 under the great Earl Strongbow, and he soon reached Dublin. In Ulster, however, the impact of the Normans' coming was not felt immediately, but eight years later Henry II, King of England, granted to John de Courcy as much of Ulster as he could take into his possession. De Courcy was quite a character, and he had many military accomplishments. He was tall and fair-headed, strong and energetic, and he often saw it as his duty to command in the thick of battle. He rode a white charger and was careful to fulfil an ancient prophecy about the appearance of the conqueror of Ulster.

His rule was a period of revival in the fields of administration and agriculture. He built many churches and castles such as had not yet been seen in the province. He later became Earl of Ulster, and after five battles and several narrow escapes he conquered a large part of the north-east. In 1180 he was ruling over one-sixth of all Ireland. He now held one of the many seigneuries in Henry's territories.

One of his priorities was to develop and secure the Irish territories for Britain, rather than to trade via Dublin. With a view to this he built many castles in Counties Antrim and Down. This was the greatest concentration of forts anywhere in Ireland, except Wexford, in Norman times. In County Antrim Dunluce Castle was fortified, for it held a position of great natural strength on a flat-topped rock which had been occupied since early times. Dunluce Castle lay fifteen miles west of Rathlin Island, on the mainland coast. The castle is separated by a deep gully some forty feet wide from the neighbouring cliffs, and could only be reached by a drawbridge. Underneath is a sea cave with a boat harbour and an entrance on the land side.

The fortunes of Dunluce Castle are closely linked with the history of Rathlin. Dunseverick, five miles east of the castle, was another site which de Courcy improved. It is also likely that he occupied Donananie, which lay immediately south of Rathlin.

The seaport of Brittas now comes into view. The name

'Brittas' is believed to have been derived from the Norman word *'bretasche'*, a wooden palisade. On the east coast of County Antrim de Courcy founded Glenarm, but his principal fortress was at Carrickfergus, where there is an immense stone keep. It was to remain a stronghold of English power in Ulster throughout the next six centuries. Even today, with a lot of construction taking place all round Belfast Lough, the great keep of Carrickfergus is the most striking building along the lough shore.

In 1180 John married Affreca, daughter of Godred, King of Man – a wise diplomacy. The year before Godred had sailed with over thirty ships to help the Irish besieging Strongbow at Dublin. He escaped when Strongbow turned the tables on his enemy. Affreca's brother, Reginald, who succeeded his father as king in 1186, was described in *The Orkney Saga* as a great Viking, Lord of the Western Isles. For three winters he stayed upon his ship without entering a smoky house. Port Mananann, the landing place of the Manxmen, is shown on old maps of Rathlin, recalling the visit of Reginald and his Norse brother-in-law. De Courcy, who was back in favour, obtained the lordship of the seas with powerful Viking allies. This was an important measure, for de Courcy started to rule Ulster like a king. He struck his own coins, making and breaking his own barons.

Island monasteries as a whole were out of fashion, but two cathedrals, five monasteries and 190 churches are recorded as having been built by the great earl. The religion that followed de Courcy's establishments was English and Rome-centred. De Courcy wanted to secure the churches on Rathlin. He had great energy and enterprise and he must have visited the island, appreciating its religious importance as one of Ireland's largest sea islands in a remote part of his lordship.

The castle known as Bruce's Castle, near the north-east corner of Rathlin, was built during the reign of King John, which coincided with the later part of de Courcy's reign in Ulster. This fortress has been the scene of drama out of all proportion to its size. It is a castle of considerable natural strength, with the inner keep sited on top of a rock stack eighty feet high with sheer walls on every side, separated from the mainland by a gully of sixty feet. The building was about the size of a squash court. There was also a gully at Donananie on the mainland at Ballycastle. The drawbridge led to the outer bailey, which was rectangular, seventy yards by fifty yards. The south and north sides used the natural cliff for protection. On the west side was a deep artificial ditch. Today only a length of the north wall of the keep and a corner of the bailey are to be seen. Many additions and alterations were made over the centuries.

There is a flat rock on the seaward side where boats came to land, and south of it is a cave where the boats could be pulled up. The west winds blew gales, but boats could anchor off the castle in safety for most of the summer. From the walls the isolated north-east of the pyramid of Torr Point can be seen to the south. A sea chief could see it from his bedroom window. The castle was built with mortar, fired with coal. Some portions of the mortars are now in the museum at Trinity College Dublin. Dr Hamilton first reported this curiosity and described the material as 'seacoal', but this does not indicate that it is a different substance from what we know as coal. When there was a fair wind, coal was transported great distances across the sea.

Dr Hamilton visited Rathlin at the end of the eighteenth century, when the coal users were occupying Ballycastle. In the south of England, coal was only gradually becoming used shortly after the reign of King John. Its use on Rathlin Island indicates an unexpected degree of technical advance. This is typical of de Courcy, who could have picked up the idea on one of his visits to London. De Courcy's other castles in Ireland show a similar use of coal.

In 1205 Hugh de Lacy, the viceroy, turned King John against the conqueror of Ulster, whom he much respected. De Courcy had been deposed from the earldom and de Lacy took his place at a time when King John was forced to sign the Magna Carta in England to respect the wishes of the barons. A short time later de Lacy had overstepped his powers, which King John had outlined for an Ulster earl. John arrived in Ireland to put the house in order. De Courcy accompanied the expedition. John was outside the walls of Carrickfergus when the castle surrendered. He learned that de Lacy and his wife had fled to Scotland by boat, and he sent de Courcy after them. They were captured by Duncan of Carrick, a member of the family of the Earl of Galloway.

Resettlement of lands followed King John's three-month 'blitzkrieg'. Duncan of Carrick was given large grants of land in north-east Ireland in return for his help. As well as capturing de Lacy he also assisted Lord Grey, King John's justiciar, in a fight on the Inishowen Peninsula, lying between Lough Foyle and Lough Swilly. He brought a fleet of seventy ships.

Rathlin went to Duncan's kinsman, Alan, Earl of Galloway, in a grant of 1213. Confirmation deeds of 1215 and 1220 called the island Rachrunn. In passing to the Galloway family Rathlin again became for a short while part of Scotland, as it had been in the days of ancient Dalriada. It was ruled by sea kings of Viking blood. In the final year of his life, in 1216, John, however, restored the island to the de Lacy family. The de Burgos, who had ruled Connaught, married into the de Lacy family. Four years later Rathlin changed hands as part of the fief of Richard de Burgo, Brown Earl of Ulster, who had been the son-in-law of its former owner. Rathlin was too remote to be efficiently ruled by the Brown Earl, and he let it out to tenants who were not really domesticated.

Chapter 7

The Consolidation of the Middle Ages

The year 1242 is important in Rathlin's story. John and Wallace Bysset, members of a Scots family, were accused of the murder of Patrick, Earl of Atholl, at Daddington. Patrick was a grandson of Alan of Galloway, who had owned Rathlin for a short period twenty-six years previously. The Byssets came to England with the Normans and had ties with Scotland, where we find the name spelt as 'Mysett'. The family is said to have been of Greek origin. When Patrick, Earl of Atholl, died in his castle at Rathlin the four brothers were summoned to Edinburgh. They said they were not interested in holding Rathlin, but their servants had been seen in the vicinity. They had decided to make a run for it. They fled to Ireland where some of the family had become established and had acquired from de Burgo land in the Glens of Antrim (or the Glynns, as it was known). The lands were to be held in the family for four generations. In 1279 it was found by inquisitors that John Bysset, son and heir, was the first John to have stepped upon Irish soil. He held his lands from de Burgo for a rent of £4 8s. 5½d.

It is not clear how often the Byssets occupied Rathlin, but perhaps very little. Their main castle was down the east coast of Ireland at Glenarm. The Byssets were having trouble with their subtenants, for in a history of seventeenth-century Ireland it was written that in 1374 the Scots made a successful raid on the Irish mainland. Now Sir Randal de Burgo and Sir Eustace la Poer entered Rathlin, burned cottages and put the inhabitants to death. Counting the Viking attacks, it was Rathlin's fourth massacre.

During this period Scots pirates raided the island and seized the castle. They mistreated the inhabitants, who consisted of MacDonnells and Blacks. They were dealt with very harshly, and they had to bring daily provisions to the castle. Turlough Mac Ilene (Anglicized to Charles Black) conveyed the provisions. At the usual time the people were sent to cross the drawbridge and passed time in the castle until the evening. The chief and his entourage feasted as usual in the hall while their prisoners looked on. They were uneasy in their seats and conditions were cramped. Turlough and his brave followers played a waiting game. At an arranged signal they leaped out, dirks in hand, and killed all the enemy. The castle became the scene of great bloodshed. After liberating the islanders they set the castle on fire.

The building of the castle was quite a feat, and it is hard to understand why they burned it rather than returning it to the owner. Perhaps they regarded it as a symbol of the power of the Byssets of the mainland, where they were detested as much as the Scots invaders.

At the start of the fourteenth century Sir Hugh Bysset ruled the Antrim coast, but he still took an interest in Scots affairs and the struggle for kingship that was going on in Scotland. Robert the Bruce was the main candidate for the crown, and he needed a hideout for the winter months at a time when his fortunes were low. Sir Hugh remarked to him that he (Sir Hugh) had a joint place for him if he came to the islands. If Bruce lost the day, he could say that the invasion of Rathlin Island was nothing to do with him.

Robert the Bruce was not the first to seek refuge from his enemies on Rathlin Island. He wanted to free his country from the yoke of the English. Like other great warriors of the period he was descended from a Norman family. He laid claim through his grandfather to be King of Scots. However, Edward I of England was in favour of John Balliol, and he was crowned in 1292. Robert the Bruce had a number of struggles against the English. It was not until 1306 that he began to lead his country against the English king. Earlier that year he slew one of Balliol's chief men, the Red Comyn, during a meeting in a church at Dumfries. He declared that he had killed the Red Comyn, and one of the men replied, "I'll mak' siccor." Edward now declared Bruce an enemy of both the English and the Scots kings, and an outcast from the Catholic Church.

Bruce gathered his supporters together and marched on Scone. Here he was crowned king in March of the same year. He was, however, defeated badly by the English and had to escape to Saddell, a stronghold on the Mull of Kintyre, where he made an ally in Angus MacDonnell Og of the Isles. Angus advised Bruce not to tarry. Bruce passed on to Dunaverty, a fort at the south of the Mull, and arrived at Rathlin in the autumn of 1316. He was accompanied by Sir James Douglas and Sir Robert Boyel. The men of Rathlin were at first troubled at the appearance of such a large army of outlaws and drove their cattle for safety to a strongpoint.

This was an age of great bloodshed in Scotland. William Wallace, the year before, had rebelled wearing a sword scabbard made from the skin of a slaughtered English tax collector. Wallace was eventually hanged, drawn and quartered. Providing shelter for outlaws was a risky business, but the islanders had not much room for argument against Bruce's forces of three galleys and 300 men.

It was on Rathlin Island that Bruce planned to renew his struggle for the Scottish crown. He watched a spider in a cave near the castle, and seven times the spider started to weave its web from one wall to another on the roof. It only succeeded on the last attempt. It is difficult to discern why Bruce should have chosen a cave only accessible by boat in calm weather. Maybe the castle was overcrowded. Bruce, it is said, rowed around to the cave so that he could obtain peace and quiet to plan for the summer's campaign. Maybe at this time the King's men traced Bruce to Rathlin; according to tradition, he fled from there in a small boat and hid until his enemies were gone. The castle is now in ruins, but it is a monument to one of the great periods of the island's history. There is no evidence that Bruce built the castle; however, his men did some masonry work to pass the winter days. Bruce at this time was thirty-two years of age, and he lived in the knowledge that he would perhaps lose the Scots throne.

With the help of Angus MacDonnell Og he collected a force of thirty ships to be commanded by Douglas when the campaign season started. This is the same Douglas who was later to be the hero of one of the most famous stories in the medieval tradition. He was faithful to Bruce for twenty years, and when, in 1329, the King died, Douglas carried out Bruce's wish to be buried in the Holy Land. The ships docked at a Spanish port on the voyage, and there Douglas responded to a cry for help and joined devout Christians in a battle with the Moors. He charged into the heathen army carrying a silver casket containing the heart of Bruce. He was slain at the moment of victory.

Douglas was first to leave Rathlin, and he won a victory at Brodick on Arran, where there is another Bruce's Castle, complete with another spider.

One thing led to another as far as Hugh Bysset was concerned. Robert the Bruce triumphed and gained the Scots throne, and a few years later there is a story that he needed Hugh's support, along with that of Edmund, Earl of Carrick in Galloway. Bruce landed at Larne on 25 May 1315, with the victory of Bannockburn behind him. All seemed to be going according to plan. In May 1316 Edward was crowned King of Ireland, and Hugh with several of his family were his right-hand men. Robert the Bruce travelled to Ireland to support his brother in the campaign of 1318 at Faughart; Edward was defeated and killed. Sir Hugh Bysset had therefore backed the wrong horse. He forfeited his lands (including Rathlin) to John D'Athy.

The Byssets were not to be victimized. After a few years in exile they obtained the return of the lands from King Edward II. By 1400 the Byssets were in a position of influence. The hand of Margery was sought by John Mor MacDonnell, who was descended from Somerled and a son of the first holder of the great title 'Lord of the Isles'.

Margery had considerable personal charm, and she was heir to the Lordship of the Glens, which ran from Larne to Ballycastle and included Rathlin Island. Her father died in a fight with a neighbour. The territory of the Glens is great in extent, still very much the same as it was in the Middle Ages.

Chapter 8

The Later Middle Ages

Dean Munro wrote in 1549 that upon the coast of Ireland, four miles from the Antrim coast, lies a land called Rachlaine that was held by the Clan Donald of Kintyre. It was good land, inhabited and fertile.

The MacDonnells had married into the Bysset family, and during the following 100 years they increased their hold upon the island and North-East Antrim. The land was much more fertile than the Scots isles proper. They had changed their name to the Irish spelling; however, spelling remained the prerogative of the writer. It was sometimes written as McConnell. There were marriages into the great Ulster families of the O'Neills of Tyrone and of the McQuillans, who held North-East Antrim. A strong castle, part of which stands today at Kinbane Head, a mile west of Ballycastle, became their Irish headquarters. The hosts of the isles were ever warring with their king. There were major setbacks in 1429 and 1475, but several attempts at settlement took place. There was hope of peace for everyone. The mainland remained loyal to the people of the isles. Treaties did not last long. Refugees came to Rathlin as the MacDonnells' fortunes ebbed and flowed.

In 1470 Angus MacDonnell emerged as leader. He had courage and a handsome figure; he was learned in history and was known for his great hospitality. Many people followed the Lord of the Isles, and they might have secured their independence for many generations. Unfortunately, in 1490 his career came to an end when he was stabbed to death by Irish rebels; it is said that he was buried by his enemies. With his death the unity of the Lordship of the Isles fell into confusion, for his successor was an old man, unable to control the situation. In 1493 the policies of the isles were brought before the Scottish Parliament by King James IV. The lordship was declared forfeit and the title came under the Crown.

The fighting did not stop. The people of the isles now elected their leader as the rebellion of 1504 loomed. Donald Dubh, a son of Angus, was born after his father's death. He showed tenacity of purpose. He allied himself to Henry VIII of England, whose ambition was to control all of Ireland and Scotland as no English king had done before. Donald Dubh sent out 4,000 men and 180 galleys to help the English forces in Ulster. He left a large number of men in Scotland to fight against the Campbells when they rose up. His sudden death brought his ambitions to an end.

During the year of rivalry between the clans of Campbell, led by the Earl of Argyll, and the Lord of the Isles, the rivalry had been building up. The MacDonnells were still the most important clan, but the Campbells generally took the royal part. Many battles and murders in the many feuds had taken place over several hundred years. James MacDonnell of Islay, however, was shrewd. He kept clear of the Donald Dubh rising and made a pact with the Campbells. The pact was sealed by the marriage of Agnes, daughter of the third Earl of Argyll. He rose to become head of the clan upon Donald Dubh's death. He realized his ambition of making large additions to his Irish possessions.

It appears that Rathlin was held by the McQuillans for a period in the early sixteenth century. However, this cannot be safely established. A Norman family who had adopted Irish ways ruled North Antrim or the Route. The Route lay west of the Glens of Antrim to the district of the River Bann. Dunluce Castle took a leading part in affairs of the time. The borders of the Glens and the Route altered little with the passage of the centuries.

Piracy was big business in the North Channel during the fifteenth century. Wool and wines were carried in English ships to most ports of the continent, to Iceland and to Southern Ireland. However, merchant ships still had to shun the north of Ireland because of the risk of capture. The pirates do not seem to have been the MacDonnells, but they may have carried out the seizures with the MacDonnells' consent or Rathlin may have been used as a base. Sailors from Italy had a great interest in reaching Irish shores and were prepared for piracy. Rathlin achieved a startling position during the fifteenth century. Charts of the area were produced in Venice. Rathlin is called Ragrani or Ragran, and is drawn with an amount of detail out of all proportion to its size. Other islands appear as a blur, but Rathlin Island appears as a distinct triangular shape. Navigators were interested in any information about anchorages. The charts can be seen today in collections, but they were not available to the public to any great degree at the time when they were first drawn. It is probable that a great collection of Venetian glass was obtained at Rathlin or at Ballycastle. A glass industry flourished at Ballycastle from the eighteenth century.

One hundred years of Irish history has been lost at Rathlin because of the Scots chieftains' ability to hold out at their leisure. Accurate records were not kept. Then a new group of contenders for Irish territory came upon the scene. They kept records and have provided us with detailed accounts of the restless years following 1551 – the English had arrived.

Chapter 9

The Sixteenth Century

It has been said that Rathlin Island was the greatest enemy Ireland ever had. From about the year 1520 James MacDonnell of Dunnyvey and Islay started to extend Scots influence, together with his brothers, Colla, Alexander and Sorley. Scots colonies were to be extended into Ulster, forming an important force from the River Bann to Glenarm. James had been brought up at the Scots court, where he learned to write and quickly absorbed the arts of diplomacy, but he did not take part in the rising of 1543. This earned him unpopularity. At the time he belonged to the junior branch of the family, and was elected Lord of the Isles.

The title had become illegal, but he kept the support of the royal party. Agnes Campbell was to be given in marriage. In this way she could win the friendship of her clan's traditional enemies. As well as being a competent diplomat, James was also a sailor and fierce warrior. For the first time the Lordship of the Isles was governed by the family, but it was not interested in an Irish colony.

The next brother, the great Colla, was bow-legged as a result of his long hours in the saddle – he was a great horseman. James had appointed him Captain of the Route, or North Antrim, and of Rathlin. He lived most of his time in Ireland, where he held the castle of Kinbane, except for one incident in 1551.

The colonists fought hard to be equal to the McQuillans. They raided and expanded into the territory of the O'Cahans and O'Neills. Ireland resounded with the song 'The Heather Isle', their battle cry.

Tradition states that Colla raided against the O'Cahans along with the McQuillans of the Route, and they were invited to spend the winter at Dunluce Castle. Colla now had the affection of Eve McQuillan, daughter of the head of the clan, but he had to escape with his men from the Route when a plot by McQuillan was discovered. Colla headed for Rathlin and found that it was uninhabited. He had to live on cattle's flesh during his stay. This points to the fact that in these years Rathlin Island was almost solely a fortress, and that there was only a small resident population. The Scots made more use of their residences on the mainland at Waterfoot, Donananie (lying west of Ballycastle), Kinbane and Dunseverick.

In these years Rathlin was governed by the Lord Deputy. There was also the more important post of Lord Lieutenant; the only difference was that the Lord Lieutenant could quit the country without the King's permission, whereas the Lord Deputy could not.

Ulster and Ireland in these years appeared to the average Englishman as remote as China, a country where there were no Ten Commandments. It was rather like the Wild West in the nineteenth century – a land of opportunity, but impending death. The hardships of fighting were great. For the Irish and Scots the most successful tactic was to avoid battles other than those which were necessary. The object was to continually harass the English, cut off stragglers and intercept food supplies – in other words, to fight a guerrilla war. The English commanders retaliated by burning the Gaels' corn and killing their cattle. It was a dirty war. For troops on active service, breakfast consisted of a handful of meal mixed with some cold water, and the food was eaten with the point of a dagger. There was little food or shelter from the winds. There was also a trade in spices, wines, whiskey and beef. For the ordinary sailor there were no luxuries, and they looted and stole wherever they had the chance. Death as a result of sickness was as high as thirty per cent in some campaigns.

With the English hungry for expansion in Ulster and the rest of Ireland, trouble was inevitable. Rathlin was bound to be the centre of attention. It was until the 1550s that the English Government became concerned about the Scots as a powerful and growing element in Irish politics.

Sorley Boy MacDonnell, the youngest brother, was captured by Sir James Crofts, the Lord Deputy, and was held prisoner in Dublin. In 1551 the Lord Deputy, accompanied by Captain Cuffe and Sir Ralph Bagenal, set out for Carrickfergus to attack the Scots. They had four ships and several hundred men. It was the first time in many years that the Lord Deputy had come so far north. The colonists drew near the north coast and they revealed methods of torture that had not previously been recorded.

King James now turned his close attention to the events on Rathlin. He had enough boats to land 100 men on the island, but not the 300 to 400 which he estimated were required to kill the Scots on Rathlin. It seemed a good idea to capture some of the Scots galleys that had been drawn up or anchored off the east coast at Port Sassenach ('the port of the Englishmen') near Bruce's Castle. The land force proceeded to march and to wait at Ballycastle while Cuffe, commanding the English ships, approached Rathlin and anchored off in the strong tides which lashed the island. They were a difficult target for the Scots gunners, and they did not come close to hitting them. According to the Lord Chancellor, one of the English boats set out for the shore, but it sank in a sudden swell. There was a light, favourable wind, but perhaps visibility was so poor that they misjudged the swell. Cuffe probably attempted the landing against naval advice. There is a tendency for soldiers and sailors to misunderstand each other, and Elizabeth's commanders were afflicted by this failing at times. It is clear that James and Colla MacDonnell seized the chain attached to the stranded boat, and all the crew were captured or killed. In the exchange of prisoners that followed, Sorley Boy was released from jail. *The Annals of the Four Masters* record that every man that landed was killed, except the commander. They do not mention who was involved, but the number involved indicates a more shattering defeat than Cusake admits.

We now learn something of the persistence of Sorley Boy,

who became famous as Captain of the Route, or North Antrim, upon the death of his brother Colla, seven years later. Sorley was now aged forty-five. He was an experienced soldier and had led the clans on a number of occasions. He was fifth in line of descent from Margery Bysset. His name was a Gaelic version of his forebear, Somerled, founder of the Gaelic Lordship of the Isles. Sorley was so called because he had yellow hair. He was shaggy, tall and broad-shouldered, and he wielded his two-handed sword in battle with the agility of a young man. It was said of him that he walked like a strong buck and looked like a lance at rest.

Sorley now raided Carrickfergus to celebrate his freedom, and the next year he carried off the constable of the castle.

These events took place in 1551 and 1552, and mark the beginning of a period of thirty-five years of war, with varying fortunes between the English and the MacDonnells, the McQuillans, the O'Neills, and the Donegal O'Donnells. There were also numerous inter-clan marriages, which make the task of writing history more difficult.

Rathlin now had a key position as an offshore island base. As long as the Scots held the island, they could raid the mainland when they liked. Sea power was important and England controlled the seas. The chief fighting strength of the Scots lay at Kintyre and the isles, where there were always enemies. The strength of the Irish colony depended upon the Scots' ability to reinforce Rathlin. The Scots ships were antiquated – 500 years behind the English ships – but in the narrow waters they had an advantage. The larger ships boasted ten oars and could carry 100 men. The smaller ships were known as *barlinns* or *birlougs*, and they usually had six oars. The galleys may have been designed after the style of Viking ships, for they were pointed at each end. They had a single mast amidships, with a Viking-style square sail, and a chieftain's banner at the bow. Few other details have survived. Pictures show them as having a few coats of arms. There is a crude sketch scratched on a stone wall at the entrance to Dunluce Castle. The galleys could make the trip from Ireland to Scotland in almost any weather.

They travelled fast. A signal from the top of Fair Head would summon about 2,000 men from Kintyre within several hours. The weakness of the Scots ships lay in their light construction and they were not able to stand up against heavy gunfire. The most experienced skippers avoided, if possible, encounters with the smallest English ships.

The English Government was short of money, and as a result there was a shortage of ships. There was also a lack of harbours and landing places. There was no harbour between the River Bann and Larne, where a steep-keeled ship could shelter for the winter. This also applied to the Kintyre Peninsula in Scotland. Scots galleys, on the other hand, could use any creek or beach, and the galleys could be pulled up into safety. In calm weather the Scots, with their ability to row, could oppose the English ships without being first attacked. The English attempted to counter this advantage by sending up smaller craft known as brigantines in 1563. *The Makeshift* and *The Post* were oar/sailing warships which were capable of carrying several light guns and up to sixty sailors. However, they had a short range and were difficult to manage in stormy seas. They do not seem to have achieved a great deal. In 1575 Essex brought similar light ships which were of great use.

From about 1562 onwards it was customary to have one royal ship on the coast. As the war proceeded, ships were sunk. *The Saker*, the first of the Irish galleys, was succeeded in 1572 by *The Handmaid*, a newly built ship of ninety tons. She was succeeded by *The Popinjay* in 1587 and *The Tramontana* in 1601.

The Scots were strong on the land, and Sir Francis Knolls, in 1556, said that there were 300 Scots compared with 600 Gaels. The Gaels had no seafaring ships at this time, other than a small fleet on faraway Clare Island on the west coast of Ireland.

Crofts undertook two other expeditions against the Scots, but neither was effective enough to reach Rathlin. His understudy, St Leger, did little better. In 1553 the Scots, under King James, laid siege to Carrickfergus Castle for several weeks.

In 1556 the Earl of Sussex was appointed Lord Deputy of

Ireland, and had as his captain his brother-in-law Sir Henry Sidney. In 1577 Sir Henry was able to land on Rathlin in a more organized attempt than that of Cuffe. He slaughtered the entire population. One account claims that a son of Sorley assisted Sidney and was rewarded with a gold-mounted sword and spear for his enthusiasm. There is little mention of the massacre in *The Irish Annals*. The incident is generally covered up by historians because of the size of the effort. Sussex followed up this success with a raid on the MacDonnell lands. Flying his pennant, the Royal Staff, in *The Mary Willoughby*, a ship of 140 tons, he sailed up the Clyde and burned James MacDonnell's castle of Saddell on Kintyre, destroying all the MacDonnells' archives. Then he raided Arran, but as a result of bad weather he was unable to raid Islay, Gigha and the lesser isles.

The History of Carrickfergus mentions the raid of 1558 and says that a garrison and colony were set up on Rathlin by Sussex. Sussex lost one ship on the rocks during a storm and this appears to be the earliest known shipwreck upon the island.

There was no attempt by the English to hold on to Rathlin very long. Sidney estimated that it would cost £300 per year to maintain a force on the island – too much for the royal finances.

Sidney was an English aristocrat, a refined courtier, good and witty, a great conversationalist, a competent soldier and an able administrator. However, he was also a cruel man, and extremely ruthless. His son, Sir Philip, accompanied his father on Irish expeditions, but earned more praise as a poet than as a soldier. He felt a need of this to obtain social equality with the Lord Deputy, his brother-in-law, who had served four terms in Ireland. He was expensive to hire and perhaps he could have served more continuously and obtained a reward. He did things on a grand scale and travelled with a large retinue. Elizabeth received him at court, but she could have hired a cheaper man. He has been accused of gluttony and treachery.

Several maps and accounts of the period suggest that Sorley Boy built a castle called Donananie on Rathlin near Bruce's Castle. This is confusing, for he had a stronghold of that name constructed some years later on the mainland cliff just west of the site of present-day Ballycastle. Elizabethan maps also show a rock called Dunelhuny sited off the coast of Rathlin near Doon Point. There is no detailed information about the rock, but perhaps the old fortification on the point was called Castle Voodish. Sorley Boy had an Italian lieutenant, who acted as his advisor on fortification. He was probably responsible for the fortifications on Bruce's Castle and at Donananie.

In 1558 Queen Elizabeth ascended the throne of England. In the same year Colla MacDonnell died at Kinbane, as also did Conn Bacagh (the Lame), head of the O'Neills. His last works concerned the security of his clan. He was worried that they might become English, sow wheat or build a stone house. His son succeeded him – Shane O'Neill, a passionate man of the sword. The Irish nicknamed him Shane the Proud. James appointed Sorley as Captain of the Route.

When Queen Elizabeth came to the throne her policy was to support Shane (whose sister was Sorley's wife) against the Scots. She was perhaps influenced by the MacDonnells' victory at Aura in 1599, giving them the edge over the McQuillan clan for some years. This would clearly leave them room for expansion if unchecked. Sorley Boy commanded the MacDonnells in battle, and when he was charged by enemy horsemen he retreated over a path of rushes he had secretly laid down in a bog. The horsemen charged at the gallop, tied to the saddle in accordance with custom, but they floundered into the bog and were quickly slaughtered.

James MacDonnell was confident that he would regain his Irish territories. He built himself a mansion, reputed to be the finest in Ulster, at Red Bay on the Antrim coast.

Now the Queen was interested in an English plantation in the province – a second 'Pale' in North-East Ireland. One of her advisors was John Smyth, who remarked that Ulster and Connaught were quiet, and that Rathlin should be taken from the Scots. Twenty-five soldiers were to be stationed there in the castle that Sorley Boy now occupied, for Rathlin was a major stumbling block for English colonization. There the Scots brought their spoils and kept them there until a flight to

Scotland could be arranged. He said that when the Scots left their homes to make raids upon Ireland it was inevitable that they would make much mischief. The Queen decided to have galleys ready to combat the Scots of the isles. The galleys would sail to Olderfleet (Larne) Lough, the River Bann, Lough Foyle, Lough Swilly, Sheephaven and Esroy (Assaroe). This would keep the Scots from plundering and fishing in the River Bann and other locations in Ulster.

Elizabeth's plan was sound, but little could be done about it until the power of the MacDonnells was combated. Shane, relieved of the presence of the Crown forces and surrounded by an efficient intelligence service, succeeded, in April 1568, in picking a moment when the clans were drawing in their crops. Sorley Boy had only 400 men holding the Route, or North Antrim. Shane O'Neill burned the MacDonnell house at Red Bay and there pressed the Scots, whom he outnumbered two or three times, and carried on up the coast to Glentaisie, the glen of the two rivers, which meets the sea at Ballycastle. James MacDonnell, upon seeing Sorley Boy's signal, returned it from his house; he gathered together a few men and jumped quickly into the first boat available. He told his brother Alexander to gather forces and to follow as soon as possible.

It was a slow passage for the wind was blowing in a south-westerly direction, but at length he had contact with Sorley Boy. His fortune was not sufficient to prevent the battle, which began at five o'clock the next morning, from ending with a victory for Shane O'Neill. There were about 500 dead on the Scots side. Among the few survivors, James was severely wounded and Sorley Boy was captured. Shane was a timorous man and could not believe his good fortune. The Lord of the Isles was his prisoner, begging for relief for the price of all his lands in Ireland and Scotland.

Rathlin played a minor role in the conflict which culminated in this bloody battle. It was a stopping place for Alexander, who arrived with nine galleys, 100 men in each. But he was a day too late. He thought he might attack, but this might mean death for the prisoners. He sent a number of officers as a ransom, but O'Neill said it was for Queen Elizabeth to decide Sorley Boy's fate. The problem was solved by the death of the Queen.

In his obituary in *The Annals of the Four Masters* he was described as a stalwart fellow, a fine, munificent man of many troops.

James and Colla were now dead and Sorley was still a prisoner, and the territory of the Route passed to Alexander.

Shane now proceeded to capture Dunseverick and laid siege to Dunluce Castle. To effect surrender he told them that Sorley Boy would be starved until they gave in. After three days Shane massacred them. He had received his Scots prisoners – twenty or more in number. Shane now proceeded to lay siege to the English stronghold of Newry. Defeat followed upon the presence of Sidney and the Donegal O'Donnells. Shane now released Sorley Boy and sought refuge with the MacDonnells, commanded by Alexander of Cushendall on the Antrim coast. This seems to have been a madman's act, but perhaps he was desperate. A great dinner was held to celebrate this apparent union of the clans, but both sides became heated with drink and a fight developed. Shane was stabbed to death. James was avenged and another phase of the Irish Troubles had come to an end.

Once Shane was dead, Elizabeth once again looked upon the possibility of an Ulster plantation. The Scots now reoccupied much of their lost land. Elizabeth dispatched Captain Piers, Constable of Carrickfergus, to conclude a pact with the MacDonnells, signing over Rathlin and the lands that lay beyond to the O'Neills on condition that the MacDonnells evacuated the Route and the Glens of Antrim. Sorley appears to have honoured his part of the bargain. He kept most of Ireland for five years; then he became occupied with family feuds on the Mull of Kintyre.

During the truce a remarkable event took place on Rathlin. In July 1567 there was great feasting to celebrate the long-awaited marriage of Turlough Luineach O'Neill, Shane's cousin and successor, and Lady Agnes Campbell, widow of James MacDonnell. She was very cultured, speaking English, Greek and French with great fluency. Bagenal found her to be a very noble and wise woman. Her dowry was 3,000 Scots Redshanks, who were Scots mercenaries. The Queen sent Captain Thorton to intercept the trade at sea, but he failed. The bridegroom made a good bargain. Sorley Boy presided over the festivities and there had not been a greater event in Ireland since 1,500 years earlier. Their castle was of considerable size and was able to accommodate twenty-five people. Sidney had been to the mainland to arrange for repair to the walls and to attend to other details for the shelter of the guests. The marriage was probably carried out on the site of the present-day parish church – sacred ground on the island.

There was gossip about the newly-weds. Argyll, the bride's brother, had sent Turlough a present to celebrate the occasion, but the bridegroom refused to accept it.

At this wedding the Scots would have worn multicoloured garments, and wielded two-edged swords which hung from the shoulder. (The kilt was introduced into Ireland by a road contractor 200 years later as a more suitable working garment.) Some would have boasted polished longbows with leather strings and quivers of arrows that whizzed in flight. Turlough's gallowglasses would have had an axe along with other offensive weapons. The chief had flowing curls, a yellow shirt dyed with saffron, short trousers and a fur cloak.

Among the guests at the wedding was Fion, also known as Ineenduv, Agnes's dark-haired daughter. She had been betrothed in the same agreement to one of the O'Donnells of Donegal and in a short while was to become the mother of Red Hugh, one of the great leaders of revolt in the sixteenth century. Ineenduv is one of the most famous characters in Irish history.

The high prows of galleys reared their heads, colourful with the banners of the chieftains, and anchored in Church Bay in a semicircle. Storytellers and jesters were present, and all the trappings of a Celtic court, including Highland bull-baiting, horse racing and much drinking of whiskey (usquebaugh).

There was little romance in the marriage between the groom and the bride. A middle-aged widow, Lady Agnes had a flat-topped mansion built on Crocknascriendlin, in the valley east of Church Bay. She had in her possession the finest apple trees in the north of Ireland. However, she may not have spent long on Rathlin for she went to live with Turlough at Dunslong Castle on the Foyle. She now started to intrigue with the Scots and English courts on behalf of Angus, her son by James.

Chapter 10

Troubled Times

In 1553 Walter Devereux, Earl of Essex, arrived. Aged thirty-four, he was a gentleman of the highest honour, and he had all the trappings of an aristocrat. During the first contest with the Irish he exhibited generosity, but this was taken as a sign of weakness. In time his confidence was undermined. He became sad and harsh.

Captain Smyth's half-hearted attempt at administration had left the English colony in Ulster in such a state that Essex, the Queen's favourite, had had little difficulty in persuading her to revoke Smyth's grant and turned the position over to him. He had to meet expenses out of his own resources to launch the plantation and to equip the armed forces necessary to support and safeguard it; this was in return for greater lands at Farneny in County Monaghan and at Island Magee in County Antrim, near Larne. Sidney had four ships to enforce the law: *The Saker*, *The Hove* (a small barque), *The Makeshift* and *The Post*. Essex had to raise his own men and solve the problems he encountered in an effective way.

The Queen appointed Essex Governor of Ulster with much wider powers than his predecessor. The change was not of any consequence as far as the Scots were concerned. Elizabeth included Rathlin in her gift to Essex and the territories were earmarked for colonization. Only six years before he had allocated much of the island to Sorley Boy in the agreement created by Captain Piers and the government. Sorley had carried out his side of the bargain. The inclusion of the island in the grant appeared to be a flagrant breach of faith.

Essex at first met with reverses. He suggested to Elizabeth that she make a pact with the Scots, permitting them to reoccupy the Glens, but Elizabeth refused to do this. There were reasons for her decision: hatred of her cousin Mary Queen of Scots and fear of her release from custody to compete for the English throne were on Elizabeth's mind.

By 1575 the Elizabethan plantation of Ulster had begun. As far as Rathlin was concerned, it was not surprising that some planters revolted. The Scots were outraged at the loss of their property as well as by the agreement made with the Queen. Grants had been offered near Carrickfergus, but the planters had given up and had returned to England.

As for Essex, the difficulties in carrying out the scheme had been made much greater by the jealousy of the Lord Deputy, Fitzwilliam.

Elizabeth wrote on 22 May 1575, outlining her proposals and insisting that the Scots should be kept in their place, but her supplications fell on deaf ears. The Queen also told Essex that she had for some reason changed her mind. She frequently changed her position in regard to Ulster, and it depended on the advice of Berkley (Essex's close friend) and the Earl of Leicester (an even closer friend of Essex's wife).

Leicester's task was to keep Essex occupied as far away from London as possible. Essex was not permitted to make plans, and he did not seek the favours of Elizabeth. Leicester enjoyed her charms – and there was also the beautiful Lady Essex, with her white arms and red lips. Leicester wanted to marry the Queen. In the summer there were revels at Leicester's great house in Kenilworth, where Elizabeth was well entertained. As a queen she enjoyed much success with the English court and she looked upon Rathlin as an attractive island in the North Channel.

Essex now had a change of mind that would affect the people of Rathlin. Walter Devereux was frustrated, blaming everyone for his misfortunes. He was deep in thought and planned to hold his lands distant from England and from Elizabeth. Funds had to be raised for the Irish project.

Devereux now lost his reputation as a soldier and administrator; he was close to losing his wife to a man he hated. His ambition was to be Lord Deputy of Ireland in place of Fitzwilliam. The only chance he had of escaping from ruin lay in ensuring that he obtained the Irish estates which he had been half promised. To obtain the estates he had to regain Elizabeth's favour. However, each failure had been reported to her and exaggerated by his enemies at court. The bold, formerly successful Essex would be reduced to bankruptcy and to selling his family estate at Penshurst. This might reduce him to a landless man. It was a terrible situation. He now wanted to be back in Elizabeth's favour.

At the end of June Essex made ready to carry out the Queen's final instructions, which would entail leaving Ulster as peaceful as possible. He had to cover up the failure of the plantation, or colonization of the province. Essex had made a treaty with Turlough Luineach O'Neill, which covered the western part of Ulster in a line along the Bann, so that they would be safe on the east side.

Sorley Boy went out to meet Essex, so that the inland territories could be assured. A garrison of forty men was left on Rathlin Island to stand against a serious English attack, but he could not possibly hold on to Rathlin all the time for there were 400 men in the vicinity. There were also three well-manned English ships on the coast. There were now more men on Rathlin than at other times. Harvest labour came from Scotland.

Sorley Boy and Essex met near Coleraine. Essex had wanted to increase the chances of victory, but after the first few days of fighting the Scots forces were proven to be inferior. They returned to the forests, leaving only a few Scots to watch the English camp. Essex rampaged through the countryside for many days. It was found that, due to another gale, the ships ordered to sail up the River Bann were not able to get across the bar. Essex's forces used up their rations, so they had to call off the campaign. There was another setback. With his own forces Captain John Norris (whose father held the station of Groom of the Stole and had been executed almost forty years before for alleged adultery with Anne Boleyn, Henry VIII's second wife) now took the field. Norris liked the colour of court life and the outrages and ruthlessness that prevailed. He was subject to great mood swings, but he had progressed in the royal forces. He sympathized with Essex.

In the camp, the night before the forces were ordered to withdraw, they hatched a scheme for their mutual advancement. They were forced to hold out at Rathlin, and they were in a good position regarding sea power. The ships failed to arrive in the River Bann so they returned to Carrickfergus. The capture of Rathlin would have little or no strategic value, but a report might be created to make it look important.

Next day Essex fell back southwards. He did his best to draw Sorley Boy after him and to keep him as far away as possible. He wrote to Elizabeth on 22 July from Dundalk, giving her a colourful account of the land operations with no reference to further projects for attacking the Scots. Sorley Boy now wanted peace. It was best not to spoil any good news. Nine days later, on 31 July, Essex had every reason to be in a state of excitement in describing what happened after he left his camp near Coleraine. He marched south with the main force and ordered Captain John Norris, Constable of Belfast, with 300 soldiers and eighty horses, to return to Carrickfergus in order to reinforce the garrison there. Secret instructions changed hands upon his arrival at Carrickfergus. Norris called upon the captain of the frigate to confer in de Courcy's great castle. The ships were anchored off the town. It was to be decided whether the weather was suitable for a row up 'The Rathlins'. The flagship was called *The Falcon* and it was commanded by one Francis Drake. The frigate had been brought back by Drake from the West Indies and bought by Essex. Frigates were of shallow draught and light construction, and it was planned that they could take advantage of the heavier ships and overlook the Scots galleys. They entered the harbour carrying 200 soldiers.

Essex wrote to Elizabeth about Norris's secret instructions in respect of the frigate captain. No one knew better than Francis Drake how to run a combined operation and how to make an emergency landing at dawn. Only the year before he had succeeded after several failures in capturing a Spanish treasure convoy on its way across the Isthmus of Panama to Nombre de Dios. He was aged thirty, and already an outstanding figure. He had taken part in one expedition which he did not like, and then there were several more expeditions, one after the other. He had established a reputation and earned the adulation of his fellow townsmen. He returned to Plymouth, with his holds full of Spanish gold, on a Sunday morning; and when the whisper went around the pews in the church that Sir Francis Drake had returned, the whole congregation left their seats in the middle of the sermon. They ventured down to the quay to welcome him. The treasure was important loot for England, though the country was officially at peace.

Burghley, Elizabeth's advisor, had to overcome diplomatic difficulties with Philip II of Spain. He sent Drake to Ireland to assist Essex and to lie low for a couple of years. When he was off duty he must have dreamed of his round-the-world trip, which began in 1577.

The frigate's captain gathered all the boats together that had anchored off Carrickfergus Bay on Belfast Lough. The large ships were towed astern. They sailed out on 20 July. They found that the winds were favourable, and the flotilla became separated on the sixty-mile voyage up the coast, a journey that took twelve hours. They managed to rendezvous forty-eight hours later on 22 July in Arkill Bay, on the east side of Rathlin, but they were solid fighting men.

Now the islanders proposed to resist the landing. Essex commented upon the activities of the islanders and sent reports to the Queen.

Drake had a considerable reputation for being independent. On his round-the-world voyage two months later he said that gentlemen must haul and draw with the ordinary sailor. He probably oversaw the installation of the great culverin situated in Church Bay, west of the fort, where the ground falls away for hundreds of yards to a boggy depression. It was protected by an earthen bank from the Scots bowmen. From just above the gun Norris and Drake could look down upon the outer courtyard of the fort. They could see that it was protected by the North Channel.

They directed their gunners to concentrate on the breaking down of the gate. By the afternoon of 25 July a breech was made. Norris's contingent made their assault and fought their way over the drawbridge and through the gate, but they were unable to bypass several barricades of wood inside. Two soldiers were killed and eight wounded, but the losses on the Scots side were much more serious. The captain of the island fell, and three of his men fell with him. Six others were wounded. There was now a garrison numbering forty fighting men. The English retreated to their own lines, not disappointed with the afternoon's work. In the evening they succeeded in setting fire to the wooden ramparts, and it became clear to the islanders that there would be an assault at dawn which they would have little chance of repelling. There was no well in the castle, and 240 souls were crammed into an area about the size of a doubles tennis court. There was a shortage of water and fuel. There were no guns with which they could reply effectively. Their only hope lay in delaying for as long as possible in the hope that a strong wind might scatter the English ships, or that Sorley Boy would make a diversion.

The July night was short and there was no sleep for those within the walls, where women and children outnumbered the fighting men by four to one. Two or three days before the barefooted soldiers had come within sight of a shot from the English, they had fought mock battles with one another using swords and bows. They lived in constant dread of the enemy. The women attended to wounds, and helped in gathering up soil and stones to repair the defences.

A quarter of a mile to the west, just out of sight, was the English camp. To seaward, in the half-light, the dark shape of a frigate could be seen. The crew were alert and her guns were ready to prevent any escape. The other boats could be seen occasionally as they patrolled to the north-west of Rathlin, guarding against any reinforcements from Scotland.

The Scots cried out: "If only Sorley Boy would come! If only he were here!"

The defenders of Rathlin must have known that there was little or nothing that could be done in the face of the greater numbers of Drake's men and his patrolling ships.

In the fort, however, there were still some high spirits. They were determined to shed as much English blood as possible. Others were for making a deal with the Sassenach.

The constable climbed out over the walls, saying that he wanted to talk. Norris, however, would make no guarantee even for the safe return of an envoy. The walls were slippery in the darkness. The bargaining was long and drawn out. An hour later the constable returned white-faced to announce that he had agreed a truce. The constable was to be handed over and the garrison was to lay down its arms and have a safe conduct back to Scotland. The troubled defenders could not believe such good news. A few soldiers were placed upon the walls, but the others were able to rest from their duties.

The dawn came and Norris came forward to claim the constable. It was arranged that all arms were to be placed at the gate; then the people were to come out and surrender, moving towards the ships that were waiting in Church Bay.

The constable with his wife and children went first, accompanied by his own hostage, Alexander Oge MacDonnell of the Glens of Antrim. This boy was being held by Sorley Boy to ensure his father's good behaviour. The constable's party were led away separately.

After this separate groups proceeded over the hills, out of sight of their comrades, and they were then surrounded and butchered – men, women and children – by English soldiers. The bodies were stripped of their garments, along with any other articles of value, by the English soldiers who would later sell them to supplement their meagre pay. Some of the bodies were cast into the sea, and others were placed in large common graves dug by captives at the point of a sword. The English troops were efficient, but most would not have liked the slaughter. It was said that they were mortified.

Silence fell over the fort, which a few hours earlier had been the scene of violence and emotion. Later that day the soldiers were divided into parties, a large one to garrison the fort and repair the defences, and others to search everywhere the Scots might be hiding.

A line of soldiers three or four yards apart was drawn up, stretching from one cliff to another across the width of Rathlin. Boats that were keeping pace with them along the shore landed parties to look into caves. The enemy were hauled out, stripped of their possessions and slaughtered.

Another group rounded up 300 cattle, 3,000 sheep and 100 stud. The soldiers now gorged themselves on mutton.

A few days later the ships withdrew, leaving a garrison of eighty men in the fort. If Norris kept his side of the bargain with the constable, his wife and child were taken away with him. He had to spend a while in jail.

It was sound military tactics to divide a garrison against itself by offering good terms to those who would surrender. In 1608, on Tory Island, the Governor of Ballyshannon granted McSweney his life on the condition that he surrender the garrison with seven men dead within it. This McSweney did immediately. The same conditions obtained at the island in Lough Beagh, County Donegal, in the same year.

A secret deal was in Norris's mind when he insisted that the constable should recognize the Norris clan, but the constable had a terrible choice. He did not like to put his wife, his child and himself at the mercy of the state, but the alternative was death for all in the fort, plus a few English soldiers.

Essex's letter to Elizabeth described the victory, and another letter from Walsingham also outlined the position.

Sorley was in the Glens of Antrim, and he rescued some of the men of Rathlin Island. He is said to have run berserk when he witnessed his kinsmen being massacred. He said that he had lost all that he ever had.

The other Scots chieftains were in a similar state. They had hurried back a day's ride from Glenconkeine ready for action. They stood upon Donananie Castle, from where they could see

The Falcon and her consorts at anchor, and also cruising along the shore. They heard gunfire and saw boats plying to and fro, and landing parties to search the caves. There was the smell of smoke, and they watched as little groups dashed across the green uplands in search of refuge. The Scots enjoyed a feeling of importance as they helped to provide rescue parties, but the wind brought them under the guns of the English frigate. They already accounted for eleven ships afloat during the operation. Sorley Boy decided to try to take Carrickfergus Castle. In this way he hoped to draw off the enemy for a time. Sorley wanted revenge.

There are a number of versions concerning the raid, and it is clear how Essex planned it and carried it out. Its military value was almost nothing.

Sorley Boy wanted to be kind to his women, children, animals and freemen. Now he would have to hold the Mull of Kintyre.

There was, of course, much greater change on Rathlin than on the mainland. In view of the English power at sea, if for some reason he wanted to leave the families of leading members of the clan on Rathlin for a while, experienced soldiers would have had to be brought from Scotland with reinforcements for Rathlin's protection. None of Sorley's sons or wives were on the island. The daughters are also accounted for. If one of them had been killed in the raid, Essex could hardly have resisted informing Elizabeth. Why were the chieftains not mentioned in the report? If they had been taken, why were they not held as hostages for ransom instead of being massacred? In Walsingham's letter there is no other mention of captains. It is not known how many pointed the sword at the English; Essex perhaps invented the number of slain.

Miskimmon in *The History of Carrickfergus* records the number at 240 – a more likely figure than Essex's. It is likely to have come to his attention through the reports of sailors, who had no vested interest in doctoring the total number of dead. Essex mentions hostages or pledges in his report to the Queen, who took a great personal interest in the island. The running-mad of Sorley may or may not have been an invention, but the fact is that his report must have been exaggerated in regard to the number slain. It is likely that Rathlin had a small garrison, their families numbering perhaps about 150 with a few resident crofters and a body of harvest labourers. There were movements of people to and from Rathlin, and there were reports of the rustling of livestock. Today Rathlin has about 1,000 acres of arable land, and a recent count tells us that Rathlin has nearly 800 head of cattle. Recording the history of Rathlin is like trying to solve a jigsaw puzzle.

The massacre has lived in memory. In the Irish wars prisoners of lower social status were usually massacred. Life was not valued in Elizabethan Ireland/Ulster. When a force of Irish kernes were used by Henry VIII, their methods of warfare were criticized by the French king. Military conduct was not generally observed in situations like that of Rathlin Island; however, one might have expected better from Essex. The ferocity of the Rathlin massacre stands out as one of the most terrible events perpetrated by the English upon the Ulster Scots and Catholics generally in Ireland.

The Scots started to make it over to Rathlin. They landed first with muffled oars in the darkness to search for the dead and to take revenge. One adult had survived along with a woman named McCurdy who had managed to hide in a cave. The McCurdy family still lives on Rathlin. One child also survived, according to a story told on the island. A small boy who was hiding under a wooden bench feasting on a raw *crubeen* (pig's trotter), was seen by an English soldier. The soldier was horrified, seeing a child reduced to such hunger, so he managed to get his wife to care for the boy as he grew up on Rathlin.

Numerous workmen were employed to repair the castle at a cost of £37, according to the priory records, but some civilians refused to take the risk of visiting Rathlin. Norris bought a dinghy for unloading commodities, and this additional service cost a further £60.

Autumn approached and every night or two a sentry on the walls would fall back choking with a Scots arrow through his throat. When foraging parties were sent out, they were liable to be wiped out. In the end, the garrison had to rely on food and water arriving by sea. The ravens and crows on the cliffs at Rathlin did not now lack prey.

Sorley now had a new plan. Many of the forces that had taken part in the Rathlin expedition had returned to Carrickfergus Castle, and just six weeks later Sorley was out at the head of his forces, mainly composed of kinsmen of the Rathlin victims. For the first time in the history of Ireland, a strong English garrison was assailed in its own fortress. Captain Baker and 100 soldiers who had taken part in the raid were killed. Sorley carried off all the cattle, but Carrickfergus itself was preserved.

The events that followed are a testimony to the persistent nature of Sir Henry Sidney, who was now back in Ireland for the fourth time. He had a compelling influence and was a great one for fair play, and he was able to influence the events of the time. He took over from Fitzwilliam as Lord Deputy, and landed on 22 September with Sir Philip on the Skerries. He recognized the terrible consequences which might follow from the Rathlin massacre. He set out with only 600 men, and reached the Glens of Antrim early in October.

Drake and his crews had been paid off, leaving no naval force in the area, but Norris remained responsible for the island's garrison. He was in a reasonable frame of mind when he heard the news of Sorley's approach, and he agreed to meet him. Sidney, remaining sensitive to the old man's grievances, withdrew the garrison on Rathlin. He gave Elizabeth the lame excuse that the castle had no well. This appears to have been good enough to please her.

Essex was made Earl Marshal of Ireland for life – not just 'at the Queen's pleasure', as was usual. His grants of land were confirmed. He did not live long in his high office, for he was only just appointed when he fell ill. He died on 22 September the following year of dysentery after a long agony of three weeks, during which he remained a religious fellow. Some said he might have been poisoned, but it is more likely that he died of natural causes. Leicester now abandoned his efforts to become a consort to Elizabeth.

The Queen had liked Norris as a young gentleman, and he was older than Essex. He was now thirty-nine – not reckoned to be youthful in those days. Boys of fifteen were matched with women. He perhaps had a special relationship with Elizabeth. Captain Piers said that the Queen turned to him when her life was in danger. The Lord Deputy, Crofts, finished his days as Comptroller of the Royal Household. Norris was knighted and appointed President of Munster for his part in the Rathlin raid. Peace was maintained until 1578, with the exception of a minor raid. He left Ireland for ever, a poorer man than when he had arrived.

Chapter 11

Rathlin Is Conquered

John Price wrote to Walsingham on 1 May 1586, saying that Rathlin was a desirable place, full of heather and rocks, but there was no wood on it.

As a result of Sidney's peacekeeping activities, Rathlin remained in Scots hands, but Elizabeth became suspicious. *The Handmaid* and *The Achetes* were commanded to stop and search all Scots ships except those chartered by the corporate towns of the mainland.

A new turn of events took place with the arrival of a certain Captain Crawford (who supported Sorley Boy). With the consent of Argyll, he set about the fortification of the island. However, Edinburgh denied any knowledge of the matter. An unusual aspect was that Crawford's force was described as being made up of 'inland Scots' and men from the Scots isles.

King James IV was only fourteen years of age, and Sir Nicholas White believed that Turlough Luineach was preparing to capture the King and bring him up as a foster-son. This was unlikely for there were strong movements afoot in the kingdoms of Scotland and Ireland to remain independent. Agnes O'Neill, née Campbell, Turlough's wife, had been to Stirling to negotiate with the Scottish Government.

Rathlin was not in the news again until 1585, when Sir John Perrot, one of the most busy Irish Lord Deputies started yet another raid against the Scots. He is said to have been an illegitimate son of Henry VIII, and he was respected and liked by the Gaels for his fairness. He was, however, criticized by Elizabeth. The move into Ulster was perhaps an effort at justification.

As the land party marched slowly north, *The Handmaid* and *The Achetes* were sent ahead with instructions to intercept the Scots if they attempted to escape by sea. Captain Thorton was in charge, and they captured six Scots galleys on passage. They missed others in the Foyle Estuary by a few hours. Thorton, the commander of the Irish galleys, and in effect Admiral of the Irish Sea for in the region of thirty-one years, is perhaps one of the most interesting characters of the century. He was first arrested for piracy in *The John of London* in 1561, but somehow he kept his neck and joined the royal service – a turncoat move. It would perhaps have been symbolic if he and his men had sailed in one body through Rathlin Sound. None of his logbooks have survived, but his sea and land commanders had nothing but praise for him, for he would effectively put into action all policy. He obtained his reward in an age of injustice and disorder, and retired with a royal pension, being granted lands near Limerick and the post of Provost Marshal of Munster – all for services at sea.

The royal ships were easily identifiable, but the flat-bottomed hulls were not as effective in the troubled waters of Ulster than they were in the Mediterranean.

Perrot came below Dunluce Castle and marched ten miles west of Rathlin on 15 September 1584. He succeeded, with Thorton's help, in mounting a culverin and two brass sakers in the rocks near Dunluce. A culverin was a large gun that weighed 4,500 pounds and fired a seventeen-pound shot with a six-pound ball. Calm weather was required and good seamanship to get close to the rocks at the foot of cliffs. There was no port nearby. Perrot threatened the garrison's survival, but Randal MacDonnell boldly remarked that he would hold out. Perrot started his bombardment, and after a few days the castle was captured; but everyone in it had been killed as a result of the siege. Among the booty was St Columba's pectoral cross of gold, 1,000 years old, possibly the most prized possession of the Scots clan.

Perrot now planned a follow-up attack on the island, but like most expeditions to Rathlin it had to be postponed because of the weather. The Lord Deputy was concerned about the continuing good weather so that he could get food to the island. The Lord Deputy landed a large force on the north coast, greater than was usual for this time of the year. Up to 2,000 men had to be victualled by sea. The ships landed on the beach at Ballycastle. In their correspondence the commanders congratulated Perrot and asked about conditions. The sea was often too heavy to permit the employment of boats. Supplies had to be drawn in on a long rope on rafts guided by sailors wading up to their necks in the cold winter seas. The defenders were glad to see the no-man's-land of Rathlin Sound.

On 1 January 1585 Sir William Stanley was summoned from Munster in the south of Ireland; he then marched his men from Bushmills to Ballycastle. It was planned that within the next two or three days he would meet Henry Bagenal, his cousin, who at this time was at Glenarm. He was able to make a pincer movement to dispel the remaining Scots forces from the Antrim coast.

At Ballycastle he found Captain Carleill encamped at Bonamargy Abbey with forty-seven soldiers. With him was Captain Warne, commanding a troop of men. The forces were stabled in the nave at Bonamargy, which had a thatched roof. The horses had to be trained for the coming campaign, and their commanders must have been pleased at the prospect of getting them undercover during the frosty nights. Bonamargy was the burial ground of the MacDonnells of Antrim, but the monks had been cleared out a good many years before with the dissolution of the monasteries by Henry VIII. It was at this time a stone building. The ground around Bonamargy runs down to the River Margy in the west.

Captain Bowens with his company were allocated quarters at Donananie Castle, about a mile to the west. Sir William Stanley was tired after a day's march. What neither captain realized was that the night before a strong force with horses had rowed across Rathlin Sound and landed a few miles down the coast of the mainland. They had avoided being seen by English ships and by wood kerne – the light troops that Perrot used for scouting.

An hour before midnight there was a full moon and a flight of arrows was the first sign of attack. More arrows followed shortly, and horses galloped up, carrying men with long staves and bundles of burning tow. They thundered into the camp and before long they had got on to the roof of the abbey. The abbey quickly caught fire. Sir William had been fast asleep in his tent when the attack started, but he now rallied the defenders. It was a curious scene. In the firelight under a winter moon the clash of swords sounded, and the yells of the Scots mingled with the cries of the islanders, especially in the abbey. Sir William was wounded in the back by an arrow.

The Scots kept up the attack for about an hour, and they succeeded in killing three of the soldiers. Sir William still led his troops, but he was again wounded – in the arm, the side and thigh. The Scots standard-bearer was killed at the head of the attack.

Twenty-one Englishmen were wounded and three died. Seven horses were burned to death in the abbey, and the cavalry equipment was destroyed in the fire. Sir William had to obtain replacements from *The Hove*, a barge lying off in the bay.

On the same night, a few miles to the south, another Scots force attacked the company which was coming up to meet Stanley Bagenal (according to Captain Lane). He saved his own neck by a flight back to Carrickfergus, and there were comments about his behaviour.

Sir William wrote his account from Donananie three days after he had recovered from his wounds. Perhaps the atmosphere in the abbey had cast a spell upon him for he converted to the Catholic Church a year later. This soldier now became a traitor, taking his company over to the Spanish side at Deventer in the Low Countries.

The raid upon the camp was just the sort of attack the Scots could launch in an effective fashion as long as they held Rathlin. They were helped by the wintry conditions. A few weeks later a party of fifty-two of them had anchored, and as the result of an intelligence-gathering exercise every one of them was slain, including Donald Ballagh, the captain who had played a leading part in the successful attack upon Carrickfergus Castle nine years before.

Two days after the attack on 4 January, twenty-four galleys from Kintyre were seen passing Ballycastle; they must have been an impressive sight in the calm weather, and the wind played a decisive role. It was estimated that there were about 2,500 men on board the galleys. Sorley Boy was in command, and his fleet landed at Cushendun. His Scots had ample resources.

The attack that took place on Rathlin was at the beginning of March. It was early in the season for combined operations. The formidable force commanded by Sir Henry Bagenal included his nephew Ralph, Sir William Stanley, Captain Henshaw, Berkley (Arthur's son) and Savage. They swept through the Glens of Antrim, but they found few opportunities for fighting. They reached Ballycastle on the 9th. The Scots did not attempt to hold the castle, which was half ruined. Crawford's attempt to rebuild it must have been forsaken.

They sent away their wives and made a stand in the old fortress of Dunmore, near the north coast of Rathlin. Fierce fighting took place, which Sorley, now eighty, engaged in. His nephew Donald Gorm was wounded. On the English side Sir William Stanley was again wounded. The young Ralph Bagenal distinguished himself and he thereby recovered the military reputation of his family. This was the second visit to Rathlin by the Bagenals.

Two brothers, Nicholas and Ralph, had first come to Ireland from Yorkshire in 1542 in order to avoid a charge of manslaughter. They received a pardon from Henry VIII and both were knighted. Ralph became a member of the Privy Council. Nicholas, the Marshal of Ireland, acquired large amounts of land.

Sir Henry Nicholson's son, who commanded the 1598 attack, succeeded his father as Marshal, but he was killed in 1598 at the Battle of the Yellow Ford in County Tyrone.

The Scots had nine galleys prepared at Doonigiall. When the pressure of the English became too much, they headed for the Mull of Kintyre. It was no doubt a well-planned withdrawal to avoid Thorton's ships. Both sides deserved great credit for their gallantry in battle, but the Scots had now lost Rathlin Island for the third time in thirty years. The English captured from the island between 200 and 300 cows and some 500 sheep. A garrison commanded by Captain Henshaw, with Arthur Savage as his lieutenant, was left on the island.

The Munster poet Eugene McGrath chose to give the Duke of Ormonde credit for the success of the campaign against Rathlin. The Scots may have gained from the kindness of the English duke. There is abundant evidence to show the open-handed way in which he distributed captured cattle to his supporters, and he had foresight in gathering food supplies around Lough Neagh.

In the autumn the Scots attacked Dunluce Castle. With assistance the Scots landed in boats during the night and were hauled up the walls. The garrison was quickly defeated. Peter Carey, the constable, was driven into one of his hiding places. He had been warned by Perrot to annoy no Irish in the castle, but he paid the penalty for confronting the intruders. He was captured and hanged over the walls. There was no water, and Perrot, concerned at the loss of the castle, tried to get Sorley Boy poisoned. The attempt failed.

There was now division amongst the MacDonnells, Angus, James's son and Sorley's nephew were trying to obtain lands in the Glens of Antrim by approaching the Queen at court through the influence of a friend – Agnes O'Neill, née Campbell, Turlough's wife. Sorley was not to be beaten, but the part of courtier may not have come naturally to him. He was eighty, but as soon as he heard the news he summoned a clerk to send a letter pledging eventual allegiance to the Queen if the grant could be given to him instead. He came from Kintyre to Rathlin in a small boat, and he exhorted one of Captain Henshaw's soldiers to get the letter passed on to Perrot.

Elizabeth now realized that a great armada was beginning

to assemble in the ports of Spain, and she was more concerned about fighting off the Spaniards than she was about Sorley Boy and his Scots. In May 1585 she made a pact with the Scots and Perrot, in which Angus and Sorley were given substantial grants, including Rathlin. Sorley got Dunluce and the western part of the Route. Elizabeth was careful to include in her rents several lots of hawks from Rathlin.

This marks the end of the protracted war between England and Ulster. Sorley's wife died about 1582. However, the old man married again in the next year to the daughter of Turlough Luineach. In 1588 the Armada at last set sail from Spain, but because of bad weather had to sail north and down the Atlantic coast of Ireland, where the weather conditions spelled shipwreck and death for the flower of Spain. Sorley acquired a fortune in gold and jewellery, as well as three guns salvaged from *The Girona*, which came to grief near Dunluce Castle, in MacDonnell country. A number of survivors were assisted in their escape to Scotland, but there is no reference to Rathlin in the accounts of the Armada.

Sorley Boy spent the remainer of his years writing his memoirs and having his portrait painted. If his account is accurate, then history might be kinder to Sorley and Elizabeth. Sorley died in 1590 at the age of eighty-five in his favourite castle, that of Donananie. He is one of the most picturesque characters in sixteenth-century Ulster and he was a courageous soldier. We can sympathize with him, with his long yellow hair turned white as he fought one Lord Deputy after another, losing many battles, but never crushed. He never sought favours by false means and he finally enjoyed the twilight years of his life in North Antrim, where he had fought for for over half a generation.

During the O'Neill rebellion that occupied the remaining years of the sixteenth century, Angus MacDonnell was one of the four chiefs to remain loyal to Elizabeth. Other Scots now joined the rebellion, and reinforcements arrived from Scotland. In 1559 Captain James Carlisle, a government spy, recommended that two galleys be stationed at Rathlin to prevent the Scots reinforcing O'Neill, but the plan was not put into effect. Sir Arthur Chichester in a later letter seems to imply that he made a number of expeditions to Rathlin during the O'Neill revolt, but there is no mention elsewhere of them.

In 1603, within a few days of O'Neill's surrender, Elizabeth died.

Chapter 12

Irish or Scottish?

With the death of the Queen and the end of the O'Neill revolt a new era began in the person of King James I: it was the start of the Stuart monarchy in England. The Scots of Antrim now found themselves in a better position to ask for court favours. Sir Randal's son was knighted and given a grant of land in the Glens of Antrim that included Rathlin Island. In April 1604 James I wrote about Sir Randal's surrender of the old grant to call into existence a new age, and he was careful to include Rathlin (or Rathlyns). Carew passed on the instructions to Sir John Davey, the attorney general for Ireland. In view of the sudden depopulation of the land, the Lord Lieutenant, Mountjoy, drew up a grant but it did not include Rathlin, which was esteemed along with the territories of the Glens. In 1605 Rathlin was formally bound over to Sir Randal MacDonnell.

The Scots monarchy was still trying to annex the isles to the throne. In 1615 Sir James MacDonnell, who had been imprisoned at Edinburgh, encamped and carried once again the standard of rebellion. He joined forces with Colla Kittach McDonald, who had been plying the waters of the Scots isles as a pirate for a long time, and he commanded an impressive fleet.

Earlier in the year Colla was told about a ship sailing from Glasgow to Lough Foyle laden with salt, wine, beer and spirits. Colla sailed close to the north coast of Rathlin after much fighting and loss of life. Sir James joined Colla's forces at the island of Eigg. They enjoyed success in the area for a while. Their prime object was to free Kintyre from seven years of hard rule by the Campbells, but Argyll's forces were too strong for them. Cattle were captured while Colla made his way up the coast. Sir James was defeated on the mainland and Colla fled to Islay. Sir James came first to Rathlin, where he stayed for a few days in September, and then went on to Oronsay to try to gather fresh forces. However, resistance was futile. As Argyll's forces came into sight, Sir James and most of the leaders fled to the Irish mainland, leaving their fortunes to their fate.

Randal took no part in the revolt of his cousin, but in 1617 a legal action for the ownership of Rathlin Island was started against him by a Scot named Crawford of Lisnorris. Rathlin had been granted to Crawford's successor in 1500 by James IV of Scotland.

MacDonnell sought advice as to what country Rathlin should belong to, Ireland or Scotland. If it belonged to Scotland, then Crawford's claim appeared to be reasonable. If it belonged to Ireland, King James IV of Scotland had clearly no right to grant it to any of his subjects under any circumstances. Sir Arthur Chichester, who was the Governor of Carrickfergus, gave his opinion on the matter mentioned in a letter of 10 March 1617. It was pointed out that Rathlin lay only a league from the Ulster coast, but seven leagues and more from Scotland and the Scots islands. Further evidence was produced to show that Rathlin was part of Ireland, for the soil was the same. It was said that the soil was not fertile and did not nourish any living thing. On the other hand, Giraldis Cambrensis, the historian, wrote in 1170 that the ownership of Rathlin had been hotly disputed and it was insisted that the island belonged to Britain.

To assist his case Randal MacDonnell called upon the archivists of the time. Peregrine or Cocogry O'Duigenan, who was a member of the family who had completed *The Annals of Kilronan* and had also assisted the O'Clerys in compiling the historical records known as *The Annals of the Four Masters*, was brought to Dunluce Castle by Sir Randal. He called upon the use of the judgment of St Columba in the great Dalriada controversy of AD 575. During the sixth century there had been arguments between the colonists of the Scots portion of

Dalriada and the parent Dalriada based in North Antrim. A council at Drium Ceatt, near Limavady, discussed whether the Scottish side owed dues or military service to the High King of Ireland (the Ard Rí), and St Columba had passed judgment. The verdict was announced by Columbanus, Columba's younger colleague. Columbanus's decision was that the land occupied by the Antrim Dalriada, including the island of Rathlin, was to be considered Irish soil, and it was to continue under the hegemony of the High King. The Irish Dalriada was from that day forth allied but independent, free of all tribute or services to the parent country. This is a case in history where a colony's complaints were settled by negotiation.

Sir Randal MacDonnell visited London in his quest for historical records. The marriage between Jon Mor MacDonnell and Margery Bysset mentioned in a previous chapter gave ownership of the island to the McDonalds. King John granted Rathlin to Alan of Galloway, who was also involved in the Norman Earls of Ulster's ownership of the island. Rathlin was excluded from the settlement after the Battle of Largs.

Sir Randal's arguments regarding Rathlin were lengthy and complicated. He finished up by stating that the eldest brother, Sir James of Dunluce, had frequently been to Scotland and visited the Scots coast before James I became King of Scotland and England. Crawford's case started with quotations from Solinus, the Roman geographer whose description of the inhabitants of Rathlin was mentioned before. He mentioned that the Hebrides, or Aemonae Insulae, belonged to Scotland. Others took the same general view as Solinus – Ptolemy, Marcianus and Serephanus. However, there is a weakness in evidence that relies on the inaccurate surveys of 1,400 years earlier.

Randal now tried to press his claims using the authority of a grant of several lands, including Rathlin, by James IV to Adam Bede in 1500. This followed the surrender of the Rathlin kingdom to Jon, head of the isle, in 1593. Rathlin had not been held long by Alexander (the father of James, Lord of the Isles, and of Sorley), who was a chieftain that represented a different branch of the other O'Donnells. He would own the island by virtue of his descent from Margery Bysset, to whom it belonged as part of her estate in the Glens of Antrim.

Alexander belonged to a family that was involved in the struggles of the island kingdoms of the Scots isles, and his lands were forfeited; this misfortune for Rathlin was recorded in the Scottish papers. Adam Bede was one of James IV's most active supporters in his claim for the kingship of the isles. The MacDonnells of Antrim and sometimes the MacDonnells of Kintyre were to all intents and purposes the possessors. Bede died in 1547. Many documents had been seized, but they do not seem to have had a significance for Rathlin.

Bernard died about 1575, leaving four daughters. Henry Stewart of Barskymmen, who married the eldest daughter, established his wife's title to a share and claimed Rathlin in about 1585 from Angus MacDonnell of Kintyre. He was the son of James of the Isles, who now held his Scots kingdom of the isles. Sorley's son seized and held Rathlin.

The situation did not change until twenty years later. In 1605 Margaret and James, daughter of Aden Bede of Barskymmen and their children were received on Rathlin Island as the joint heirs of 'Ranchnie'. Now several claimants were made aware of the power of the 7th Earl of Argyll, who secretly acquired a grant in a report on the sovereignty of the island. Stewart made safe the arrangements with Argyll, and in 1606 pointed out the situation of his wife's sister. He petitioned the King in 1617 for possession of the island and said that he had done his best in his claims to the title.

The Laird of Lisnorris seems to have attached much importance to the fact that the island was reckoned by the Scots authorities as part of the Earldom of Tarbet in Kintyre (Cantyre). He said that the sheriff had made payments of its rents into the exchequer of Scotland. Amongst the many manuscripts there is a note in the handwriting of Carew, who poured scorn on the idea that Rathlin might be considered as part of the Irish territories. Crawford tried to reject Sir Randal's arguments that were based upon the situation of Rathlin, and he pointed out that the other Scots islands enjoyed a close situation.

This attack was countered by Sir Randal, who said there were extensive communities on the Scots isles as a result of missionary activities during the great age of art and learning. However, Crawford had been a notable courtier, and Randal's arguments might have been ignored and the verdict might have gone the other way. If so, Rathlin might now be in Argyllshire benefiting from the work of the Highlands and Islands Development Board.

King James I reinforced the decision by making Randal a baron. Randal was a man of many parts, and he was popular at court. He had married Alice, a daughter of Hugh O'Neill, and she had taught him the arts of diplomacy.

Crawford had picked a good time for his lawsuit. It was in the sixteenth century, more than at any other time, that Rathlin was most regarded as Scots territory. Since then Rathlin has been considered part of Irish territory.

During the seventeenth century no one had much time to worry about Church affairs on the island. In theory, at least, upon the dissolution of the monasteries by Henry VIII, the titles of Rathlin were transferred from the Abbey of Bangor to one Rice Aphugh; at a later date they passed from him to John Thomas Hibbets; and then, in 1605, to Sir James Hamilton. The title now passed to the MacDonnell, who became Earl of Antrim in the following year. The MacDonnells were now highly respected by the establishment, but there was to be more bloodshed on Rathlin.

Chapter 13

A Bloody Massacre

In the mid-seventeenth century Argyll and his men were condemned along with their associates. Shortly after the lawsuit Randal MacDonnell was created Lord Dunluce and later became Earl of Antrim. Meanwhile the plantation of Ulster was under way. Grants of land were made to settlers from England and Scotland, made possible by large-scale confiscations.

The O'Neills and the Donegal O'Donnell chiefs, facing arrest and execution, fled the country, and in 1639 there was a great rising in which thousands of people were massacred on both sides. In the spring of 1642 England made an agreement with the Scots to raise an army to help defeat the rebellion. Archibald, Earl of Argyll, was appointed commander and took the opportunity to pay off old scores with his traditional enemy Clan Donnell. He was nicknamed Grimach, or Grim. He had a squint and an expression to match.

Part of the agreement was that the Earl himself was to be made Governor of Rathlin. Rathlin had little or no importance in this land battle. Argyll's reason for seeking the governorship can only be clan rivalry and religious hatred. On the pretext of controlling the lines of communication, he sent his cousin Sir Duncan Campbell of Auchenbrech to land at the island with 1,600 troops. The intention was to kill as many McDonalds as possible. The conflict took place in a hollow in the centre of the island known as Lag-na-vis-ta-non, or 'the field of the great battle'.

The MacDonnells' forces were no more than 200 or 300

strong. There was a spot from which women watched the battle and cheered on their menfolk. It was a battle about religion, and many of the Presbyterian Scots also fought in the Wars of the Covenant. Many women and children were thrown over the cliffs in a gully now known as Sloall-na-Calliagh. This is a dark gully in the black cliffs where rocks are exposed at low water.

Stories are still told on Rathlin about the massacre. One story is of an old woman whose husband had been killed in battle. She was seized by a Campbell clansman who took a liking to her, and he carried her off to Islay as his wife. Another story is of an older woman who saved herself by quick thinking before she could be thrown off the cliffs. A soldier was watching her undress; she seized him and tossed him over the cliff instead, and he was killed. She returned to Rathlin some twenty years later, and she found her son, whom she had presumed dead. He was living in the old family farm. Another islander escaped in his curragh to one of the caves on the north side and hid there for months. A hoard of coins, dating from 1533 to 1641, found by William Curry of Rathlin, perhaps points to some pathetic islander who did not escape. Apart from a handful of survivors, the Campbells carried out a thorough job.

Up until recent times the name of Campbell was detested on Rathlin, so no one bearing the name of Campbell dared to set foot upon it. Today Campbells are well established on the island. Missions to Rathlin were sometimes a speciality of the eighteenth-century Campbell clan. In 1647, under the same commander, the Campbells attacked Islay. They captured the eighty-year-old Coll Tess Kittach, an ally of King James in the 1615 rising. They proceeded to hang him on his own ship. On the same occasion they went forth to the Mull and killed most of the population, in spite of the fact that they offered no resistance.

The head of the Clan MacLean was forced to surrender to Irishmen who were in his service. The Irishmen were hanged at once, such were the Campbell standards of the age.

After 1642 the history of Rathlin becomes less bloody. The Earl of Antrim fortified his estates, including Rathlin, as a result of his part in the 1641 rising, but they fell to Argyll and later passed to Dr Philip King, to whom the grant was made by the Cromwellian party.

The Earl regained his lands in 1662 after the Restoration. Rathlin was gradually repopulated, and Irish names appeared in the rolls of the late seventeenth century. McCurdy, Black and McCuag are names still common on Rathlin today. However, there are no MacDonnells on the island, although they were there in the nineteenth century. The earliest named tombstone on Rathlin is hard to find. It dates from the time of the Montrose rebellion of 1646, and marks the burial place of the fourth son of the Bishop of Lismore, who fled and was excommunicated for his part in the campaign. It was an unusual fate for a Protestant, but it is what the records tell. He died on the island in 1665.

There was an abundance of beef available on Rathlin, for in June 1689 a fleet commanded by Captain George Rooke in the frigate *Deptford* anchored in Church Bay and took 100 head of cattle. The cattle were destined for the besieged garrison of Londonderry. The captain was the same Rooke who later captured a Spanish treasure fleet at Lisbon and stormed Gibraltar. His attempt to relieve Londonderry was not very competent. He reached Lough Foyle on 11 June, but the starvation at Londonderry was not relieved for another six weeks. The cattle were what would be called today West Highlanders, of which there were several herds on Rathlin.

When there was a round-up most of the islanders used to take the day off and made an occasion of it. The animals had to be shot or lassoed in Wild West style. The only remains of the cattle today is a fine bull's head mounted in the manor house.

Piracy was widespread. Thirty years after Captain Rooke's visit a French frigate sailed into Church Bay to use the island as a base. The pirates mounted a lookout for shipping from a high point on Rathlin. Pirates also used other types of vessels. There was a Lookout Stone, upon which were etched drawings of sailing ships.

In a natural amphitheatre Roman Catholic services were held in the open air for fear of persecution, and a lookout was required to disperse the congregation if a stranger approached.

The altar can still be seen; a second altar was still in use after the penal days.

The first record of a Roman Catholic priest being appointed to the island dates from about 1740, but it is thought that services were held there long before this date. Bishop Hutchinson was glad to know that there were about 490 Christians on Rathlin Island. He was instrumental in getting a school opened along with a library and he instituted a phonetic alphabet for the Gaelic-speaking inhabitants. A King's County officer stationed on the island was on the board of management of the school. The process of education continued for some years, but was discontinued some time before the end of the eighteenth century. The Reverend John Martin was curate of Ballintoy. He died in 1740, and was still the incumbent at the age of eighty. A skull and crossbones symbolizes the state of affairs, and they appear on a tablet erected by his son and still to be seen at the church today.

Chapter 14

Newcomers, and Rathlin at Peace

In 1746 the 5th Earl of Antrim had managed to get himself into debt as the result of a generous personality. He was now compelled to put Rathlin up for sale, and the Reverend George Gage bought the island for £1,750. At this time he was prebendary of Aughadowey, twenty miles inland from Londonderry. His wife had inherited some money and thus he was able to afford the deal. It is interesting to speculate why a clergyman should want possession of Rathlin. He made the application when he was fifty. He was the son of Queen Anne's private chaplain. It was at this time looked upon as a wise purchase. Ballycastle at this period was looked upon as a good communal centre, and the island was recovering from the ravages of the previous centuries. In the indenture, dated 10 March 1745, which is preserved in the Public Record Office in Belfast, the name of Raghery is used. Lord Antrim retained rights of fishing, hawking and coal mining. George Gage also owned a mill, a quarry and rights to store limestone, slate and marble. Coal and salt mines were of great importance and were supervised under the direction of Mr Boyd. The mill was under reconstruction, to be completed in 1748. George Gage's attention might have been drawn to Rathlin by the marriage a few years earlier of one of his relations to a McNeill of Gigha or by the purchase of Queen Anne's boats.

Bonnie Prince Charlie, the Young Pretender, had recently planned his expedition into England. The Prince was handsome, and was popular among the people. His enterprise was one of the most daring in British history, but in April 1746, on Culloden Moor, the chance of another restoration of the Stuarts had been discarded for ever. Many of Bonnie Prince Charlie's followers fled after he had been defeated, and it is said that the Prince himself spent several weeks on the north-west coast of Ireland, waiting for a ship to take him to France. If it had put into Rathlin, he would perhaps have been greeted by many friends who would have helped to conceal him and to serve him at the risk of their lives.

Gage re-established the long tradition of Norman ownership of the island that was started by Sir John de Courcy and continued by the Byssets. His family was associated with William the Conqueror's invasion of England. The ownership of Rathlin by the Gages meant that the island would continue to provide good soldiers and sailors. They loved and served Rathlin favourably for many generations.

Gage did not live long enough to witness many changes on the island, but he might have seen the introduction of horses, solely for the use of gentlemen. He visited the island regularly, staying at Ballynoe House, now a barn. He petitioned Parliament to improve the island's facilities. He said that many ships sailed up the Irish Sea and put in at Rathlin if there was a suitable wind out to the west. Ships of 300 tons and over could ride out a gale on the east side of the island, but smaller boats were frequently lost for the want of a harbour. He said piers were to be constructed at Church Bay and Ushet, and this would greatly assist vessels in shipping coal from the colliery for use on the Antrim mainland. Cod and herring were in abundance nearby, and the piers would also be of assistance to the fishing vessels. Coal had been found in the north of the island and he said it was possible that a workable seam existed there and that it should be investigated. He asked for a king's ship to be stationed at Rathlin to counter the pirates and intercept smugglers, who were using the island as a base on a vast scale. It was said that Rathlin should be used as a public granary; great stocks of corn might be brought from the isles, where rents were invariably paid in grain. He also proposed that a lighthouse should be built on Rathlin similar to the ones in existence on Howth Head and the Copelands.

It was a satisfactory prospect, especially as the Irish Parliament had a surplus of £500 that year. Similar requests from all over Ireland kept coming in as soon as word was sent abroad. The island's case, however, was turned down and it was to be another 100 years before Rathlin obtained a lighthouse. Over 200 years later – today – Rathlin is still waiting for an adequate harbour. The Mull of Kintyre obtained its lighthouse before the end of the eighteenth century.

In the days of sail and oars the boat trip to Rathlin took four to five hours; today it takes fifteen minutes. Curraghs were in use on Rathlin until the nineteenth century; but though they remain common in the west today, they have not been seen on Rathlin for seventy years. There were a number of tragedies. One is recorded in 1772 when the rector, Mr Cuppage, and one of Gage's sons were drowned in Slough-na-more with the loss of the boat's crew.

Gage died in 1763 and his eldest son, Robert, regularly visited Rathlin, and in his later years resided on the island permanently. He had built a long two-storey Georgian manor house that withstood the storms. It stands today on the west side of Church Bay. It is a delightful sight, appreciated by many. It had a narrow corbelled yard beneath a walled garden to the west. It was built carefully into the hillside under one of the few trees to be found on Rathlin.

The shimmer from the water is a phenomenon all round the island.

Robert brought weavers to the island, and there are some remains of their workrooms. Rates of pay are recorded in the accounts book in the Belfast Public Record Office.

About 1780 the first independent accounts for Rathlin are recorded. A letter was presented to the Reverend William Hamilton, a Church of Ireland rector in County Donegal. It is said that the cultivated land was not enough. It produced excellent barley, but there were rodents. Dr Hamilton published his letters and several other literary works, but he was killed in the early part of the 1798 Rebellion.

Robert Gage may have been attracted to literary doctors that travelled the roads.

The Sheriff of County Antrim in 1787 managed to persuade the Grand Jury, which in those days possessed most of the functions of a county council, to make the switchback road that leads from Church Bay out to the west.

The islanders had great regard for Robert and his family.

Thomas Russell, who is said to have been executed for his part in the 1798 Rebellion, was a student of geology. He visited Rathlin as a guest at the manor house. He helped raise a lot of funds for the rising. A meeting took place in Bracken's Cave with the cooperation of 'Black Ned' McMullan, the parish priest. A few islanders agreed to take part, perhaps voluntarily. They made it clear that they would only do so if they did not interfere with Mr Gage and his family. A signal came from an old schooner, *The Amy*, in Ballycastle dock, but the crew was arrested and banished. Luckily the Rathlin islanders did not take part in the 1798 Rebellion, which started with high ideals and was an interdenominational movement. By the end of the rebellion there were 3,000 deaths to be accounted for.

Robert died in 1801. While his son, another Robert, was still a minor, the island was administered by an agent, who carried on a lucrative smuggling trade that did Rathlin no good. Lime was one of the principal commodities. Brandy, along with whiskey and poteen, would be collected from the boats and hidden in caves or a hideout in the houses. The contraband was later sent to the mainland.

The Blue-Eyed Maid was a famous fishing vessel of the period. It was kept in good condition and was well armed. When other vessels like it landed on Rathlin the agent would arrange for a fleet of boats to salute them. Each carried stones equivalent in weight to the contraband to be collected. These were transhipped to the smugglers, who were always ready for a swift flight. The weather might be bad, and *The Blue-Eyed Maid* in 1815 watched her consort, *The June*, being shipwrecked in a gale off the County Donegal coast.

There is a story that dates from this period, telling of a small boat lying at anchor off the east coast. The smugglers had been asleep, but the ship was soon under way and was pursued three times clockwise around Rathlin. When capture seemed inevitable they ran the boat against a rock about twenty feet high on the north side, known as Fargan Lach, behind which the hull was hidden. There was only just enough room for the boat to lie in thirty feet of water between the rock and the cliffs.

During the Napoleonic Wars the island was not affected by this twenty-year period of the French Empire. In 1808 Rathlin was mentioned in a military memoir on the defence of Ireland, which was drawn up by General Charles Dumouriz, a Republican French diplomat and soldier. He had refused to serve under the French colours and came to the British Isles, where his opinion was much sought after in view of his experience. Ireland was open to invasion for there were thirty deep bays in all its coasts. After staying with the Irish constable, Dumouriz proceeded to Larne and he said that the coast from Larne to Ballycastle was vulnerable because of its exposed position. He went on to say that Rathlin had a good bay, suitable for anchorage. A squadron based on the island in summer could patrol the whole coast of the north between Lough Swilly and Belfast. The tide is strong between Rathlin and Sheep Island and the boats could shelter from the north-west winds in the region of Ballycastle.

The general must have had scant knowledge of maritime affairs to suggest that Ballycastle was a good anchorage, and this has been confirmed by sailors through the ages. If the English ships could blockade Brest and Toulouse, as they did month after month, winter and summer, a squadron could have been maintained in Rathlin Sound. His reports point out that Ireland had few good mooring places that were suitable for the military, other than Cork, Valentia, Dublin and Rathlin. The reports say that there were stations guarding Ireland from all sides, but no naval squadron stationed at Rathlin Island.

Yachting in the Rathlin waters was becoming popular as a sport for gentlemen. In August 1816 some close relations of the

Gages set off for Strabragy Bay, on an excursion to the Isle of Jura. The captain was Robert Hanly and the boat was called *The Rambler*. It may have been borrowed from the Gages. Robert, a happy fellow, designed his own dining table a year before to celebrate Napoleon's defeat in Europe. He was married to one of the Gage women. After a voyage of about one month they reached Iona and visited Staffa.

On the way back after long delays at Port Ellen in Islay, *The Rambler* found its way to Campbeltown and eventually reached Ireland via Rathlin.

There was much traffic across the North Channel in these years – a traffic that has all but disappeared in the twenty-first century.

Rathlin had a population explosion that seems to have peaked at about 1,200 in 1784. Rathlin was ruled in these years by a benevolent landlord.

In 1820 the rector, Mr Moore, had been on Rathlin for over forty years. He had established the Bishop's library. The Protestant population was sinking steadily, but this was also happening all over Ireland. In 1820 Robert Gage, aged twenty, was appointed curate, and four years later Rector of Rathlin. This triggered a period of substantial activity.

It was necessary to suppress the smuggling, so Robert Gage arranged in 1821 that coastguards should be placed on the island. One officer and six men lived in the houses which are still inhabited on the south shore of Church Bay. This was one of eight stations in the Ballycastle area. It was necessary to improve the regulations in regard to shipping and it was necessary to confront the smugglers, and to this purpose Ushet port was deliberately blocked with boulders. The decision was reached after discussions between the coastguard officer and Robert Gage, and it indicates the extent of the problem.

In 1816 Robert Gage (the proprietor, as he was called) set aside a barn for conversion into a Roman Catholic church. It was a period of Catholic emancipation throughout Ireland. In 1829, shortly before being appointed curate, Robert had obtained money from the diocese for the erection of a new church, the old one having fallen into disrepair during the last 100 years. This building is still the parish church and was completed in 1822. It is so near the coast that the salt spray washes its walls. It is difficult to find a church in Ulster that is nearer the sea. The graveyard is still used by all the denominations, and some of the graves date back to the sixteenth century.

At the beginning of the age of universal education the new proprietors succeeded in getting a school built and a schoolmaster appointed. The church school had been discontinued for some time about 100 years earlier, and in the interim the only schoolmasters on the island had been itinerant people who might stay for a few weeks in the summer. A girls' school near the present rectory was added in 1826, and in 1834 another school was opened at Ballygill at the west end of Rathlin.

In 1822 the first six-inch Ordnance Survey map of the island was published. Studying it today is not very enlightening. A flagstaff was used for signalling the mainland or passing ships.

Robert built with great enthusiasm. He enlarged the manor house and made a large walled orchard and garden just above the upper road in Church Bay. There were trees – plums, apples and greengages. Another habitation was constructed on the north-east side of Church Bay. A rent book recorded the cash rent for each householder. In 1814 there were payments for eleven troops to the Antrim coast and one to Scotland, eleven miles from the island.

In 1837 the population of Rathlin was 1,039 inhabitants, and its area was given as 3,398 acres, including about 230 acres underwater. There was arable land of 'medium' quality. The western side of the island was 'rocky and mountainous'. Its brown rock and masses of basalt pillars are in contrast with the chalk cliffs, which, on the northern side, sweep down to the sea from a height of 400 feet, without any protective base. The soil is light mould intermixed with fragments of basalt and limestone. The valleys are rich and well-cultivated arable land, and a variety of rocky pastures are scattered over all of Rathlin. The substrata near the entrance of the island are basalt and limestone. On the eastern side Rathlin is famous for its beautiful ranges of basalt columns, differing not greatly from those of the nearby Giant's Causeway. Bands of hard chalk extend for some distance along the southern shore, and in some other places (for example, near Church Bay) they are intersected by a basaltic dyke.

Barley of exuberant quality and cattle flourish on the island. The barley was probably used by Scottish merchants, and in 1837 there was a mill for grinding oats. There was no town or village, but the dwellings of the inhabitants were irregularly scattered throughout the island.

The proprietor, the Reverend Robert Gage, was constantly resident and acted as a magistrate.

The Roman Catholic chapel is a curious building – at one time 180 children attended it.

Near the black rock on the south side of Church Bay are caverns where calcareous stalactites could be seen.

The Reverend Robert Gage is described in the *Parliamentary Gazetteer* of 1844 as being completely Lord of Rathlin. He had his own boat crew, dressed in blue-and-white jerseys, for transport to the mainland.

Dr J. D. Marshal printed another account of this period. In 1834 he founded a shop with some general supplies. He commented upon Rathlin's need for a resident doctor, for there was great hardship. Asthma and eye problems were rampant, perhaps due to the sulphurous smoky atmosphere where peat was burned in homes without a hole in the roof or a chimney. Even at a much later date smoky interiors were still commonplace and visitors might emerge coughing into the street from the island cottages while the islanders, well used to burning peat, sat laughing at the victims of the fumes.

Irish was one of the main languages spoken on Rathlin in the nineteenth century, and it was spoken there up to the 1930s. According to a survey in 1934, many of the older people spoke Gaelic. The following generation indicated that they did not wish to pass Irish along to their children.

The potato crop failed in 1847 and Robert Gage, like many

landlords on the mainland, tried not to delay helping the islanders. All rents due to him were cancelled. Many supported the Lord Lieutenant, and a Rathlin Committee was formed. One firm of London underwriters donated £10 to help Rathlin as a consequence of their honesty regarding shipwrecks. People on the island did not suffer as greatly as many of those on the mainland. They were able to rely on fish and seabirds, though they were hard to catch in winter and with a population of about 1,000 Rathlin must have been overcrowded. There were also eels, and elvers worked their way upstream to the height of the 200-foot cliffs. Through Gage's efforts there was not a death on Rathlin due to starvation, though there was undoubtedly a great deal of hardship and considerable emigration.

Clough-na-Screeve, a stone in Cleggan townland, records some of the names of the islanders who left the area for America about this time. The population of Rathlin dropped from 1,101 in 1813 to 1,010 by 1841, and then it fell to 453 by 1861.

In 1849 Robert Gage's wife lay the foundation stone of the first lighthouse to be built on Rathlin. (The entrance to Wexford Harbour had a light run by the monks as early as the sixth century, and Howth Head, off Dublin, was first lit in 1750 to guide ships on a main shipping route.) The Ballant Board bought some ground at the north-east corner of Rathlin, and here the light was turned on in 1856. It had at least two stationary lights – 295 feet and 215 feet above sea level. This was in the days before flashing lights. The lights would guide a sailing ship so that it could work its way against the tide along the north side of the island. Three cannons were used during fog until 1920, when electrical firing was substituted – shots were fired every five minutes.

In 1884 a barque, *The Girvan*, 182 feet long and 718 tons, left the Clyde bound for Aberdeen with a cargo of whiskey. It was given a tow down as far as the Mull of Kintyre. *The Girvan* failed to get under way, and on a fine sunny day it drifted on to the west end of Rathlin. Much of *The Girvan*'s cargo was bound for destinations around the island in places long since forgotten.

Only a small number of shipwrecks have been recorded in

the Rathlin histories, but there have been many. The islanders say that there were about forty on the place above a reef known as Clacken Bo, which extends west just south of the West Lighthouse. A catalogue of wrecks does not necessarily provide a lot of detail. The wrecks averaged one a year on Rathlin during the first half of the twentieth century. Sometimes very little was seen as a result of the actual disaster – only broken timber and mangled bodies were found later. In Tony McCuaig's public house are recorded a few of the ships – for example, *The Girvan* and *The Arriero* were lost in Church Bay in March 1876, and *The Cambria* and *The Saracen* were lost east of Bull Point. Many ships were lost in the fog on the north side of the island.

Other wrecks a little remembered include *The Night Scarf* and *The Bouncer*, both wrecked at Cooraghy. *The Bouncer* was said to have seen service on the Nile during the campaign for the relief of General Gordon at Khartoum.

Mrs Gage died in 1852. She had four sons and eight daughters and was in possession of an illustrated manuscript history of Rathlin. She was as talented as her husband.

The MacDonnells of Antrim do not seem to have returned to the island in any strength after the 1642 horrors, but they were shown on the roll of 1766. In 1832 there was one MacDonnell family at Ballynoe House, but by 1832 the name disappears again. Perhaps drownings in the MacDonnell Bush, or eddy, off the East Lighthouse explains their disappearance.

A boat from a corn mill at Portawillan, laden with grain for Scotland, was lost, but the date of the incident is uncertain.

Robert Gage died in 1862, having been Rector of Rathlin for thirty-eight years. He was succeeded by his son, Robert Gage, who continued to take an interest in the community and the welfare of the people of Rathlin. He kept a stock of coal, and he had a limekiln erected and assisted in the task of its building. He also improved the piers, of which there were seven on the island, none of them in good order. At Church Bay are now recorded pier sites at Killeany, Cooraghy and Portawillan, on the east side.

Robert recorded the events that had taken place about 1880

and his records have been well preserved. He also recorded the weather in great detail. He mentioned boats called *The Gannet*, *The Ajax*, *The Rambler*, *The Widgen*, *The Queen*, *The Fox* and *The Duck*. Repairs to the boats occupied much attention and one May Day he was generous enough to paint *The Ajax* green outside, white within, and black in the gunwale. The larger boats were gaff-rigged, and lay on chain moorings in the bay for most of the summer. Robert himself organized the slaughter of the Highland cattle when meat was required. The weighing of kelp, timber, grain and beer was also much recorded. For example, on 18 August 1879 *The Ada*, a sail steamer with coal for Newpark, loaded up with kelp for the return voyage.

Robert spent most of his days in several rooms in the workshop. Some visitors smelled and could not be brought into the home. Each voyage to Ballycastle has a corresponding entry recording the weather conditions. Sometimes on a calm day in winter as many as seven island boats set sail for Rathlin.

At Ballycastle Robert attended the Marshal's Court. The minutes of Poor Law meetings also recorded the activities of the shipping. Occasionally there was a visit to Belfast, but Robert would be homesick for his beloved Rathlin. He was also a doctor, and his medicine chest was preserved until recently. It contained bottles with no labels. A portrait of Robert shows a fine-looking man with a long, happy face, clad in white canvas trousers, fisherman's guernsey and red knitted cap.

Robert lived with his sister Catherine, who produced an account of Rathlin's plants. The plants included almost all the common Irish ones. The clough yellow, the snow bunting, the nightjar and the ovail were found on the island. The white-tailed eagle was once common on Rathlin, but became extinct there by 1859. The Icelandic falcon, the bean goose and the marsh harrier are sometimes seen. The Slavonian grebe has also been noticed, along with the little grebe, which is common in many of the loughs on the island. Fork-tailed and storm petrels are regularly observed on the shores. The buzzard is now common on Rathlin (four or five pairs regularly breed). The golden eagle is a rarity, but a pair of them managed to breed three times in recent years at Murlough, and they were seen once on Rathlin.

In 1864 Robert and Catherine had more birds to think about. In that year the youngest sister, Dorothea, went to take advantage of the waters at Baden-Baden in Europe. She was twenty-nine years of age, dark, tall and pretty and she caught the attention of a German prince. The family quickly took possession of her and made her feel at home. At a much later date a yacht anchored in Church Bay and was ready for a fight.

German princesses were quite well known during the reign of Queen Victoria. Prince Albrecht agreed to marry one, and they were married in the Chapel Royal in Dublin Castle on 2 June 1688. Later they had three sons and five daughters. The Prince on several occasions visited Rathlin with his wife. In 1688 his valet died, and was buried on the island. However, Albrecht later developed a taste for other women.

In 1685 the Roman Catholic Church of the Immaculate Conception was founded on the island. It is a beautiful little church of basalt with freestone trim, and it lies at the head of a very steep road up a break in the cliffs, just west of Church Bay. It was dedicated with great ceremony by D. Dorrin, the bishop of the diocese, on 22 August that year.

In the nineteenth century Rathlin was more or less self-supporting, but clothes were made from fabrics spun and woven on Scots islands. There were shirt makers and tailors as well as a 'blanket-smith'. Fish oil from 'glashans' was used to light lamps. Timber came from shipwrecks and seaweed was used for manuring the land. There was a good diet for everyone: Irish beef and mutton, with fish and duck for variety. Poteen (illicit whiskey made from barley) was available for sale. This would warm the bones on a cold winter's night. Dulce, an edible seaweed, was used as an aperitif. Fuel was scarce, since there is no peat on the island. Cow dung was also used for this purpose.

One of the main exports was kelp, an industry that was started as early as 1774. Ten years later 100 tons were exported from Rathlin, but by 1830 the number was down to thirty. The Gages accumulated kelp in a store, and now and again got a ship to collect it. All the major types of seaweed were harvested.

Women and children took to the rocks, cut the seaweed with knives and spread it out to dry. When it was dry enough to be used, it was placed in a pit with stones (in a kiln) and lighted. The dried seaweeds were fed steadily in, and anything not dissipated as smoke would accumulate as a bluish mass at the bottom of the kiln, where it was stirred with an iron rod. In the early days the price per ton was £5. It was also used for the bleaching of linen. Iodine was a by-product, and up until 1930 it was used in the making of photographs.

Houses at Ballycastle and Rathlin were shaped like beehives, but of rough stones. They were used as 'sweat houses'. A peat fire burned in the house until the walls became very hot, and clients, up to four at a time, would come to Rathlin to take part. A small air hole was opened and closed to control the temperature. Clients would be wrapped up in women's clothing or immersed in cold water. The best preserved sweat house is at Knockans, and it may be the remains of a beehive hut of great age. There is another site south-west of the gates of the East Lighthouse, beside a tiny lough.

Most of the islanders worked extremely hard for a living and they had much energy.

There were tales on Rathlin of beings intermediate between humans and the 'wee folk'. Similar beings were said to dwell on Colonsay and in other parts of Argyllshire. There is the story of Sach Bahn, who had the habit of rolling along the roads at night in a cart, and a story of a fisherman who married a mermaid.

Caban Dhu was an escheated person, and he lived on a farm in a large black house in Loch Canan in the west of Rathlin. He boasted a golden spear protruding from his chest, and he had impaled many victims. Eventually the spear penetrated his heart, and he died. The people celebrated and one room was scarcely enough to hold them.

There was a risk of cattle disease and of one's child becoming ill, and there were spells to ward off the dangers. For example, an ass's harness would be hung up to ward off the evil eye. Life was exciting in those days, even though some of the islanders never travelled to the mainland during their whole life. A visit to the mainland was full of perils.

The islanders were familiar with 'cuddins', their name for a small fish; wildfowl were known as 'forrins'.

In the old days great princesses lived on Rathlin. One was so beautiful that two lovers fought over her to the death. One of the lovers whispered to his servant – Tol Dhu by name – and the man tried to avenge them by dancing with the Princess and whirling her over the cliffs. The Princess was washed up east of Ballycastle, and from there looms the outline of Torr Head, rearing up out in the sea.

Two princesses from Islay were transformed into stones while trying to escape. The stones stand for ever off Kenramer Cliffs.

The Sea Wrack, written by Mrs Campbell in 1951, contains the story of an older generation of islanders. Mrs Campbell's mother was a Rathlin Gage and she passed most of her early life on the island. Mrs Campbell spent some time on Rathlin and she led a long and eventful life. She wrote delightful stories.

There were stories of the little folk up until Marconi arrived upon the scene. A Lloyd's signalling station was set up near the East Lighthouse for the benefit of shipping that was unfamiliar with the area. The information provided was of great importance to owners and users of ships and cargo. This was in an age when a voyage to New York might vary in length from four to five weeks. Lloyd's found that Rathlin was in a most favourable position, visible from Torr Head. A young Italian named Marconi therefore set up his new-fangled wireless telegraph system to connect Rathlin with the mainland. Marconi set up an assistant at Ballycastle in June 1898. After a number of setbacks, Kemp, the number one, looked out at the end of August for reports by radio from Altacorry to a receiver at White Lodge, Ballycastle. On 1 September Marconi visited Rathlin. He and Kemp must have been pleased with the experiments, but the equipment had to be dismantled a few days later because the Post Office blamed Marconi for interfering with their profits. They installed their own radio using a different system, but it does not seem to have worked well.

Marconi and Kemp reaped the benefits of hard work, but the

only remains of their signalling station are now at Rathlin near the East Lighthouse. Soon radio on ships would be universal and the Lloyd's signalling station took second place. The Rathlin station was closed down.

Marconi's men sighted a number of ships. The records of the coastguard station on the mainland at Ballycastle for the years 1880–85 tell an interesting tale. Riggers were still common at this time. With the close of the only British naval base in Ireland, the number of warships, submarines and RAF craft has now declined in Rathlin Sound and other waters. In 1885 there was the important sight of sails that protruded into the morning mist. There was the splendour of a full-rigged ship, heavily laden with American cotton bound for Liverpool, sailing past Rathlin's white cliffs before a full gale. The nets of a fishing lugger stood out, ready for a catch. Today the visitor to Rathlin Sound does not see the colourful square-rigged vessels of a former age.

The site of the coastguard station on the mainland is close to the old Donananie Castle. When it was rebuilt a few years ago there arose the question of another site at Fair Head. The route to the place would have cost in the region of £5,000. The station in its present situation serves a useful purpose. In bad weather it is augmented by a lookout on the north side of Rathlin. Unless it is foggy, all passing ships are under friendly watch.

Robert Gage died in 1891 and was succeeded by his brother, Major General Ezekiel Gage, who had spent fifty years in India. Because of his advanced age he decided not to take up residence at Rathlin; instead he lived at Ballycastle. He paid a number of visits to Rathlin, becoming attracted to the manor house, but a lot of his valuables were lost.

In 1902, during a storm, his eldest surviving son, Captain Richard Gage, returned from the Boer War to take up residence in the manor house and to manage the Rathlin station.

In 1810, Scott, a well-known engineer, was given the task of constructing a light on the west end of Rathlin. Here the cliffs rise 400 feet. The lighthouse is situated high up to be observed in fog. Scott overcame the problem by building a large concrete glacis at an angle of forty-five degrees on the face of the rock, with steps for convenience. The keepers dwelled in a three-storey building at the foot of the glacis.

Before the glacis could be constructed a lot of blasting had to be done, but construction was started in 1912 and the first light shone in the same year. The job was not completed until 1919. The work cost £400, a very large sum of money when one considers that an average wage was 2s. 6d. per day. The Rathlin West Lighthouse, or the Bull Lighthouse, is the only red light around the Irish coast apart from minor lights and buoys at entrances to harbours. The roar of a horn in the fog can be heard. It has been named after a field at the top of the cliffs.

Chapter 15

First World War to 2013

It was stated in 1914 that the North Channel had been so effective that it could be regarded as completely hostile to the passage of submarines. In August 1914 Britain declared war on the German Empire, and it seemed incredible that Rathlin should become a war zone. Within a month the Germans decided to mine the Clyde. The 14,000-ton liner *Berlin* was converted and dispatched to oppose the defenders. After several narrow escapes on the outward voyage the captain reached the North Channel at dusk on 22 October. The light on Rathlin had been extinguished by order of the Admiralty, so the captain was unable to steer clear of the narrows in the dark. The attempt was given up and the ship drifted seventy miles to the north-west, off Tory Island, County Donegal, where the battleship *Audacion* sank.

The German U-boats were at work. They had a range of a couple of hundred miles, and their task was to survey the British Isles where surface ships could not operate. A number of sailings of U-boats took place in the Irish Sea and the Clyde, and the Admiralty decided that barrages across the narrows were the best means of protection. Other methods of anti-submarine warfare were in their infancy. At dawn the U-boats had to dive and run the gauntlet of row upon row of mines laid near the bottom.

The waters in the North Channel were too deep and the tide was too strong for mining to be effective. It was decided to patrol a zone thirty miles by twenty from the north of Rathlin to the Mull of Galloway. When U-boats had to surface for air they would be attacked.

Rathlin became an important base. All shipping was diverted south of the island, and a light was installed at Rue Point to guide them through Rathlin Sound. In the north-east of the island forty drifters laid a system of wire nets stretching from the Mull of Kintyre to Fair Head in Antrim. The nets were ninety-six feet in depth and 2,000 yards long, and they had to hold in a strong tide. They were designed to catch submarines rather than locate them. Many types were tried. When a U-boat struck a net it pulled it away, and watching ships moved in to attack. The coastguards kept watch, supported by naval patrols. Airships bound for Luce Bay and Larne watched for the telltale signs that revealed a submarine, such as a periscope raised to spot the position of the enemy. A hydrophone station was established at Torr Head to listen for any submarines that managed to pass under the nets. The hydrophone could pick up the sound of the U-boats' propellers, but when the U-boats learned of the position of the hydrophone station they minimized the risk of discovery by taking advantage of a fair tide and running their engines at a very slow speed.

The drifters could not be expected to keep close to the shore in a winter's gale. On 28 February 1915, Wegener, a U-boat commander, had already sunk a number of British ships. He looked through his periscope, observing the west of Rathlin. He had left port three days earlier. Now he pulled down the periscope and prayed that he would have victory. He dived at the dark base of the cliffs, and he slipped through the nets. The coaster *Hatdale* avoided sinking off the County Down coast ten days later. Wegener got through again, sank the merchant cruiser *Bayani* and returned again for another conflict. During the summer and most of the next winter fear of the U-boats decreased. Wegener was sunk in August off the coast by a Q-ship.

The German submarines continued to be vigilant, for the ships were just outside the barrage. By May 1916, in spite of all the naval activity, the U-boats surfaced in sight of Rathlin at daybreak and opened up on a potato ship on passage east of Coleraine. *The Wheatear*'s captain refused to heave to. He replied with his own guns, exchanging shots near Portballintrae, on the mainland. Hundreds of people came out to watch the engagement at their doorstep. This incident has passed into North Antrim folklore. At length *The Wheatear* reached safety in Portrush Harbour and dropped anchor displaying a Union Jack on her deck. A few months later such activity would have brought many warships upon the scene within minutes. The submarines now became the recipients of countermeasures by the British.

By July 1917, Ireland had become an independent sea command with more bases than at any other time in its history. There were destroyers and up to 450 armed yachts, drifters, trawlers, sloops and motor boats that patrolled the Irish waters, all under the command of Admiral Sir Lewis Boyle at Queenstown. Under his direction Rathlin became the centre of the North Channel barrage, and 150 drifters waited for the U-boats under the command of the Admiral. There were two lines of nets across the narrows, but some U-boats got through secretly. The Straits of Dover as well as the North Channel were full of German U-boats. Through the winter and summer, day and night, about thirty drifters armed with puny guns and primitive depth charges worked in sight of Rathlin, though the area around Rathlin, where the submarines lurked, is one of the most troubled waterways in the world.

The British Isles was close to starvation when, late in 1917, the convoy system started. This marked a turning point and the rate of shipping loss dropped dramatically. Merchant ships with their convoys made ready for the Atlantic crossing, and on the return trip they dispersed into smaller convoys.

At dawn on 17 October 1917 the British cruiser *Drake*, a ship of the ocean escort that had brought Convoy HH2 from Gibraltar to the Clyde approach, held strong off the north coast of Rathlin. A few minutes later *The Drake* fell prey to the very effective torpedoes of *U79*.

The Drake had been built in 1900. Her sister ship, *Poor Hope*, was sunk at Coronel in the Pacific three years earlier. Twenty men were killed, victims of the torpedocs that hit *The Drake*. Captain Reynolds decided to head for Rathlin Sound and called upon the destroyer to escort the convoy in view of what had just taken place. Another destroyer also acknowledged his signal. Within an hour eight destroyers, with other ships following them, had surrounded *The Drake* to form an anti-submarine barrier. It was a memorable sight, even for the days when the ships of the Grand Fleet patrolled the coast. *The Drake* listed heavily as she rounded Rue Point surrounded by a flotilla of twenty ships. On board the boats lookouts strained their eyes and listened for the sound of enemy propellers.

As the ships entered Rathlin Sound there was an explosion. HMS *Brisk* was seen to be down in the head, but there was relief when it was discovered to have been caused by a mine, not another torpedo. Captain Radcliffe put in at Church Bay with a view to carrying out some repairs.

Sir Francis Drake was destined for a watery grave off a coast that he once raided, and now this large warship named after him started to sink rapidly and had to be abandoned. The crew was taken off by *The Martin* and *The Delphinium*. *The Drake* listed at anchor and its captain must have greatly regretted that he did not go half a mile further up and drive her on to the beach at Church Bay, where there would have been a greater chance that something could have been salvaged. There was a risk that the magazine might explode, so he tried not to go too close to Rathlin.

A court martial heard afterwards that the captain had been justified in proceeding alone after leaving the convoy. However, another escort for war vessels like *The Drake* had to be provided. The importance of the ships was great, for the entire force at Lough Swilly was employed protecting four destroyers.

One of the islanders recalled that he was working at the limestone cliff quarries when a large ship came in sight. He and his men ran away for fear of an explosion. *The Lugano*, a flour ship, anchored on the west of the island. Most of her cargo floated ashore.

The bottom of *The Drake* remained on the surface of the water for a while, but she later sank eighteen feet below the surface. The wreck is marked by a buoy, but in spite of this at least three ships have got into trouble there. By a coincidence, the Reverend Alex Gage, a member of the Rathlin family, had been chaplain aboard *The Drake* from 1907 to 1909.

The U-boats still operated close round Rathlin and at dusk on 5 February 1918 a liner was sunk with the loss of forty-five lives, seven miles north of Kinramer by *UB77*. A month later *The Santa Maria*, an American ship, was attacked in Rathlin Sound. Her wreck is today marked on the map close to the north of Fair Head.

During the longer days came U-boat sinkings to thwart the trawlermen in their task. On 17 April the islanders heard the sound of gunfire and the noise of depth charges. A drifter had sighted a submarine off Torr Head. The submarine heard the gunfire and submerged again, but she was finally finished off with depth charges. This was the end of *UB82*, a large submarine with a 4.1-inch gun, a machine gun and five torpedo tubes. It had a top speed of thirteen knots.

A fortnight later *UB85* fought out matters on the surface, and after another fortnight she surrendered to a trawler within sight of Rathlin. The crew were ill, and there was little fight left in them.

There were tales of U-boats obtaining supplies of food and petrol on Rathlin, and they must have sailed close to or landed on the Irish coast. Rathlin, however, was at the centre of naval activity, so this was the last place they would have chosen.

Peace eventually returned to the island and those that had served at sea came home. The nets were sold for scrap. The light at Rue Point remained, but the hydrophone station at Torr Head was shifted to Ballycastle.

After the First World War, in Ireland came the Troubles. Those who wanted the British out of the island conducted their own guerrilla warfare throughout Ireland. Rathlin was again a flashpoint and it welcomed the English as guests. A truce and treaty now followed. Rathlin and the six north-eastern counties remained under English rule whilst the rest of Ireland became independent. The population of Rathlin continued its slow decline.

In the last 150 years life on the island had become more and more difficult. Far away lay the eighteenth century, when island farmers were the enemy of their neighbours on the mainland. In the years when there were poor conditions, at Rathlin and on the mainland the small sheep farmers had to walk up to ten miles to market, but island farmers had easy access to the market using the sea. The island shore produced wrack for manuring, and the island carried on a good trade by meeting the demand for seabirds.

There was the hope of a wreck during a storm, and in the middle of the nineteenth century there were 100 a year around the Irish coast and islands.

There was a feeling that people of Rathlin Island belonged to a separate community. Apart from the earlier massacres, which were mostly confined to the Irish islands, there was a feeling that the surrounding seas provided protection. While people on the mainland had to struggle against the political odds and adverse agricultural conditions, for the people on Rathlin, the island was their entire world. There were the delights of the coffee bar and the dance floor, and there was the prospect of earning a living in the twentieth-century world. There was also the prospect of emigration for some – mainly Scots of the islands. The telegraph came to Rathlin, and was used for summoning help in times of emergency and illness, and for keeping in touch with friends.

The marine engine has taken the hardships out of boating – to which might be added the helicopter for evacuating the seriously ill. The coming of tractors, however, reduced the amount of employment on the farms.

In view of these facts it is not hard to see why the population of Rathlin has declined over the last fifty years. By 1922 a Mr Johnston, who had obtained a lease of the mineral rights until 1959, opened a limestone quarry at Killeany that employed about a dozen people to supply Glasgow. Further plans for development were envisaged. However, he got into financial difficulties and the quarry was closed in 1930. Most of the tenant farms were now acquired by the government of Northern Ireland, and were sold to tenants, many of whom are still paying the land annuity under the terms of the Land Protection Act.

Gage's estate was reduced to the manor house and its grounds. In 1966 Brigadier Gage bought all Mr Johnston's interests. What remains of the original Rathlin estate is again in the hands of the Gages.

On 1 March 1930 the Rathlin Life Steam Company was summoned at dusk to assist a steam trawler that had come ashore near Greenan Point on the north of Rathlin, in a dense fog. Visibility was down to thirty yards. The situation was saved only by rockets and the shouts of the sailors. Upon the seventh shot a line was fired directly across the ship, and by means of a buoy and a light the crew of fourteen were hauled to safety up the cliffs – one of the finest pieces of life-saving work ever seen in the British Isles. An award was made to the Rathlin team, and a brass tablet at the door of the rocket store at Church Bay commemorates the event.

During the Second World War Rathlin did not have any servicemen stationed on it. The island, however, did important work by manning an auxiliary lookout station on the north side. In bad weather lookouts are still maintained. The lighthouses were shut down by order of the Admiralty, and they were only switched on for a moment at times to guide ships coming and going. Sean O'Callaghan in a book records the existence of an illicit radio transmitter that reported the movements of shipping, but those who lived on Rathlin during the war do not believe such stories. The new lighthouse system was in operation from the beginning of the war and once again ships found their way up between Rathlin and Islay. British ships kept a lookout for German U-boats. One islander saw a midget submarine surface on the east coast. There are reputed to have been Germans at the well in Bracken's Cave, but this has never been proved.

Sorley's bones had been laid to rest in the vault of Bonamargy Abbey and there they lay undisturbed for 350 years. They were upset by robbers about 1940, looking for treasure or just lead. The remains were placed in a new casket, but this was again upset in the 1960s. Sorley Boy's bones, it was said, could be seen through a rent in the coffin.

Seabirds' eggs were a good 'finisher' at mealtimes. They provided gloss for coats. Seabirds' eggs were not mostly used for home consumption; during the Second World War many thousands were shipped to Ballycastle. In former days every farmer had the right to sections of the cliffs, which were climbed sometimes using stakes set at the top. Each ledge and cranny had its name, now forgotten. The island climbers had to have great strength and confidence. However, climbing Rathlin's cliffs depended upon the weather.

The feats of some of the cragsmen are still remembered. Paddy, a climber, reached the top of Stack An Fir Lea, which today boasts 6,200 nesting guillemots and shearwaters. They can be counted from the platform of the West Lighthouse. On the other side is Stack An Cosokey, which has a well near the top. In the nineteenth century a young climber ventured up the stack on the north side.

Rathlin's tides helped the British in a peculiar way during the Second World War. British magnetic mines were set in place. It was sometimes necessary when a ship full of weapons reached the island or anchored in the straits to regard the ship with suspicion. Rathlin Sound was ideal for naval operations and anchorage was obtained between Fair Head and Rue Point for several days. Sometimes island boatmen came out to offer assistance, and most of the sailors went to a safer anchorage.

Great were the pickings for boatmen during the war. Barrels of rum worth £70 came ashore one at a time, and at times Rathlin Sound was full of timber.

A Dutch ship dragged its anchors and was wrecked near Bull Point in 1942. The troopship *Loch Garry* landed in treacherous weather near Doon Point in January 1942 with a loss of twenty-nine lives. Other lives were said to be in considerable peril.

At the end of the Second World War an investigation was set up to examine the cost and feasibility of a reliable sea route. The Brodie Report recommended a harbour at Church Bay and improvements to Ballycastle. The total cost would be about £150,000. There were few doubts about the quality of the recommended structures. However, the scheme did not get under way. Rathlin was left in the post-war period without a good harbour.

Chapter 16

Modern Rathlin

One of the main concerns of the residents of Rathlin, and those who sang the praises of the island, was that it should have facilities like the mainland. If you visit Rathlin in the winter, making the journey across Rathlin Sound in an open boat with the spray breaking over you for an hour, you will understand the length of the passage. When there are sharp north winds, the weather on the sea can be of some concern.

There may be a dramatic fiery dawn coming up over Torr Head and its fringes, and large cumulus clouds on the opposite side of Rathlin, over Islay. At such times each hillock seems coated in gold. Standing at a high point at dawn one can see many lighthouses in clear weather – at Orsey to the north-west, with a flash every five seconds; at Inistrahull to the west, with a flash every twenty seconds; a smaller one at Shrove, at the entrance to the Foyle; at Islay; at Sanda Bay, on the Clyde; at Kintyre to the east, with two flashes every thirty seconds; and at The Maidens to the south, with three flashes every twenty seconds. In the midst of all this is the island's own set of flashes. One must now realize how close Ulster is to Scotland.

One can stand on the pier at Church Bay and see the treacherous seas that race down Rathlin Sound, and feel confinement that is like imprisonment. If there is a fog when one of the island's boats is overdue, there is an atmosphere of great tension. Gaelic mythology comes to mind as the winds sweep in. Fog could mean isolation from the mainland, and it gives the traveller time to think about what might happen next.

Since the Second World War, the population of Rathlin has been in steady decline, in keeping with other periods. In 1970 the population stood at 109, a density of twenty souls per square mile as against 130 for rural areas in the whole of Northern Ireland. Rathlin, with its heathery rocky ridges and meadows, valleys and lakes, is like an area in the Antrim Hills. Today it is mostly elderly people that inhabit the island. In 1970 only nine children were at school there, but the demand for secondary education has been added to other needs.

The island today is a self-confident community. Rathlin and its people are sound observers of its place in the worldwide community. There are advantages and disadvantages of island life.

The Gages still occupy the manor house. Captain Gage's wife died in 1947 and was succeeded by her surviving son, Brigadier Gage, who retired from the army a year later. He continued to live on the island in summer. In 1950 the Ministry of Agriculture started a forestry scheme. During the next four years 120 acres were planted – spruce and chestnut with some pine – but there was the problem of strong salt-laden winds.

In 1955 there occurred on Rathlin a snowstorm that blew across a thirty-foot open boat used by the district nurse. By this time there were a dozen cars on the island along with modern vehicles such as tractors. The first traffic accident had yet to happen. The roads were given regular maintenance with the help of a stone breaker supplied by the county council. Tyres had a short life for there was still no Tarmac. The stone breaker, all seven tons of it, had to be transported by dredger from the Foyle.

It is said that Rathlin is one of the coldest spots in Ireland for bathing, although the water might be a little warmer where the beaches shelve.

In 1957 Lord Wakehurst, Governor of Northern Ireland, visited the island.

In 1968 Robert the Bruce came back to Rathlin in the person of a descendant of the original Bruce. However, tradition states that it was only by the skin of his teeth that he managed to look after himself. Bruce's two-handed sword of hammered steel with a leather hilt is still in as good condition as on the day he wielded it at Bannockburn.

In 1960 Rathlin ceased to be a separate parish, for it was united with Ballintoy; the rectors had been on the island for more than 230 years. Today the island has only one priest of the Church of Ireland for a month in the summer. In winter, services are held once a month. The Roman Catholic Church has a presence on the island.

In 1949 the coastguard was called into action twice. The first time was early in the morning of 28 February when the trawler *Pinfall* ran aground on the rocks just below the West Lighthouse. In the darkness the coastguards, led by Daniel McQuilkin, descended the cliff, which would have been a difficult feat in daylight. By means of a breeches buoy all the crew were rescued. They were brought to Portrush later that day by the lifeboat, which was steadfast on the sea. Daniel McQuilkin was awarded the British Empire Medal for his services.

In 1962 another trawler, *The Ella Hewitt*, collided with the wreck of *The Drake* while coming into anchor. She was outward bound and the fuel tanks were full and there was an oil spillage. A Royal Naval submarine was also grounded on the wreck, while carrying out a NATO exercise. She had to be towed off by a destroyer, and both vessels damaged their propellers during the operation. The submarine commander, as a result, missed his promotion.

In April 1968 the brand-new twenty-seven-foot fishing patrol vessel *Impetus*, bound for Lough Neagh, was shipwrecked on the east side of Rathlin. The crew swam to the shore – it was a very fine night with slack waters.

In February 1921 a Dutch vessel spent twenty-one hours on a rock near Rue Point.

Rathlin has had a radio telephone for over forty years. In 1970 a twenty-four-hour STO telephone was installed, thanks to the efforts of Henry Clark, who was MP for the region. The equipment came on a car ferry from the Western Isles – two similar vessels operated between Red Bay on the Antrim coast and Campbeltown in Scotland. It managed to sail into Church Bay.

In 1960 funds were raised to help Rathlin's football team.

In 1971 it was proposed to survey the entire island from an airship. Lord Grey visited Rathlin in July.

Islay lies sixteen miles away. Its inhabitants had seven distilleries and earned more dollars per head than any other community in the British Isles.

Gigha is a very scenic spot about the size of Rathlin lying thirty miles north-north-east; its soil is similar, though not so rich. It is sheltered to some extent from the prevailing winds by a ridge of high ground along the west shore.

Islay has a milk and cream business. At Achamore House, owned by Sir James Horlick, there is one of the finest gardens in these islands, for here fine shrubs are sheltered by trees. It has been cultivated with great care over the last thirty years. Milk and cheese production have given more employment than the raising of beef.

Gigha has a policy whereby all the farmers stick to dairy farming. The milk is collected by tankers.

Jura is the next-door neighbour. It has good sailing and fishing grounds and on its mountains live thousands of head of deer, including some of the heaviest stags with the finest antlers in Scotland. Unlike Islay and Jura, Rathlin has no rivers large enough to produce water for distilling.

Compared with Gigha, Rathlin's climate seems to be a lot colder, perhaps because of the North Atlantic Drift – a continuation of the Gulf Stream that reaches the west of the British Isles and is deflected away from the north of Ireland to the Scots coast. It is therefore doubtful if Rathlin could plant famous gardens, but it was well off for milk and cheese. The pedigree beasts needed for large-scale milking were too valuable to be carried across to Rathlin in the bottom of an open boat, so the island has come to rely upon beef and fishing for its livelihood.

Many wild flowers adorn its coast, and in this respect Rathlin is like some of the Scots islands. However, many of the Scots islands have steamer piers that are used by the Royal Mail along with freight and passenger accommodation.

Rathlin, unlike many Scots islands, has an important link with the mainland, and the reader is referred to Ballycastle, three miles away. To help towards efficient farming, what was needed was a good harbour at both ends of the crossing, including a permanent berth safe in all weathers for a boat with covered accommodation. At present the Ballycastle end is often a bugbear because of heavy seas in Rathlin Sound. Sometimes one can leave the island in safety and make the crossing to Ballycastle pier; at other times it would be irresponsible to land there. Instead help is needed from the mainland. Piers and similar facilities are a better investment than unemployment benefit. A hovercraft that can run up the beaches may provide the answer, but this method of travel is costly and involved.

Today Rathlin is seen as either unspoilt or underdeveloped, depending upon one's point of view. It would be presumptuous for any outsider to dictate what should happen to it. Those that live on the island today regard it as an attractive place, but there are, of course, many shades of opinion. If a hovercraft were employed, the profits should, of course, be used for the benefit of the Rathliners. Some say that a regular flow of visitors might undermine the uniqueness of the island. Regular services might mean a flow of visitors to and from Rathlin in the months from April to October.

Today the population of Rathlin has one of the fastest growth rates in the British Isles. These islands could become a favourite attraction of the first order. The island has no hotel, but the islanders are famed for their hospitality. It is sometimes difficult to arrange accommodation. There are, however, cottages to rent on the island, and for a holiday it is just the right size. From the centre of Rathlin it is possible to take a leisurely morning stroll in any direction. The visitor will always remember this beautiful place.

Visitors to Rathlin must land on the white rocks of Church Bay, or off the old granary at Ushet Point. From there one can walk up past the harbour to the east of the lighthouse and get a lift out to the west to see the birds. At Tony McCuaig's public house one can spend a good time.

There has been much progress since 1985, which saw improvements to the harbour with an entrance basin to the east of the north pier, now well protected by rocks. Boats can now shelter all year round, including visiting yachts. The ferry service has now become regular.

When Brigadier Gage died in 1973 the manor house was sold, but the Gages still return to Rathlin each summer.

In 1987 Sir Richard Branson in his attempt to fly around the world in a hot-air balloon was forced to make an emergency landing close to the north coast of Rathlin. He presented a cheque to the islanders for £25,000 towards expenses.

Today the telegraph is an important asset and there is also a water supply at the east end. In the last few years Rathlin has acquired many other facilities. There is the 200-foot-long basin in Church Bay that holds fifty-foot covered ferries, *The Iona Isle* and *The Rathlin Venture*, which carry visitors between Rathlin and Ballycastle. Rathlin is now a popular venue for a weekend race or cruise. It is also a stopping-off point for ships sailing to Scotland.

Tarmac has been laid on the roads, water power has arrived, and there is a small windmill which kept Rue Lighthouse alight for several years. The year 1992 was marked by the installation of a power scheme on Rathlin funded by NIE and Brussels. Rathlin's rocky seabeds and stormy tides would make an underwater cable short-lived. Most island homes are now connected. Diesels are part of the scheme.

The Rathlin Island Trust was founded in 1987. Its main purpose is to provide employment for the Rathliners. Along with the manor house, there is a health centre, workshop facilities and a library. The waters around Rathlin today are not so polluted as they were in the past. Many other developments have been earmarked for the island, and its people remain welcoming and vigorous.

Oilskins and sou'westers are recommended, but yachts have continued to increase in number. The journey from Belfast or from Lough Swilly makes for an interesting holiday.

So ends my story of Rathlin, a once disputed island lying roughly four miles off the coast of the north of Ireland, and fourteen miles from Scotland.

Select Bibliography

Donald Gregory: *History of the Western Highlands and Isles of Scotland.*

Edmund Curtis: *A History of Ireland.*

E. Estyn Evans: *Irish Folk Ways.*

Hugh Alexander Boyd: *Rathlin Island.*

James Drummond Marshall: *Notes on the Statistics and Natural History of the Island of Rathlin.*

Nora K. Chadwick: *The Age of the Saints in the Early Celtic Church.*

Reverend George Hill: *An Historical Account of the MacDonnells of Antrim.*

Reverend H. I. Law: *Rathlin: Island and Parish.*

Rosemary Garret: *The Glens of Antrim.*

Stephen Lucius Gwynn: *Highways and Byways in Donegal and Antrim.*